THIRST

THIRST
OR
EAGER HEARTS

Gabriel Marcel

Translated from the French LA SOIF
by MICHIAL FARMER

CLUNY
Providence, Rhode Island

Cluny Media edition, 2021

First published in French as *La Soif; ou, les coeurs avides*
by Desclée de Brouwer in 1937

For more information regarding this title
or any other Cluny Media publication,
please write to info@clunymedia.com, or to
Cluny Media, P.O. Box 1664, Providence, RI 02901

VISIT US ONLINE AT WWW.CLUNYMEDIA.COM

ISBN: 978-1952826689

Cover design by Clarke & Clarke
Cover image: Harold Gilman, *Sylvia Darning*,
1917, oil on canvas
Courtesy of Wikimedia Commons

CONTENTS

THIRST

INTRODUCTION

by Michial Farmer

GABRIEL MARCEL, to the extent he is known at all in the English-speaking world, is known as a philosopher: as a friend and rival of Jean-Paul Sartre and Simone de Beauvoir, as the coiner of the word *existentialism* (which, like every other existentialist, he denied applied to his work), and as the producer and explicator of useful concepts like intersectionality, mass society, and the distinction between being and having, to name but a few. But Marcel's work is a kind of tripod, with his philosophical writings as only one leg. The other two—his writings on music and his dramatic works—are essentially unknown to English speakers. Very few of his plays have been translated into English, and those that have are largely out of print or available only through academic publishers.[1] Marcel doubtless would be surprised and disappointed by this development. He saw his plays as integral components of his thought, so to content ourselves with his nonfiction means understanding him imperfectly. I also suspect that this philosopher who paid so much attention to the body would want his plays to be given flesh-and-blood reality through performance, and the existing dramatic translations seem to have the page, not the stage, in mind.

I hesitate, however, to make too strong a connection between the plays and the philosophy. The temptation when reading the artistic work of a philosopher is to see it as an illustration of his philosophy. (It is of little help that Sartre, certainly the most famous philosopher/artist of the twentieth century, tended to use his fiction and drama in exactly this way.) But Marcel himself cautions us against conflating his art with his thought. Because his drama, he claims, springs from his desire to put the people around him into a dialogue that they themselves are unwilling to enter, his job as a playwright is to disappear from the stage. His plays, then, are neither Shavian problem plays nor Platonic philosophical dialogues nor Sartrean illustrations. For a play to be genuinely dialogic, the playwright must "remove[] his own personality in some way in order to provide a place for autonomous beings and their intercourse."[2] There must, then, be nothing didactic in a dialogic play, "for didacticism conflictingly implies the active and essentially indiscreet intervention of the author."[3] The playwright's job is to present an "encounter" between characters. Not only that, Marcel also claims in "An Essay in Autobiography" that his philosophical work developed quite separately from his playwriting and that "the connection between these two modes of expression did not become clear to me until fairly late—about 1930."[4] The plays can therefore be enjoyed and appreciated apart from any knowledge of Marcel's philosophy.

1. The situation with his writings on music is even more dire. As far as I can tell, there is a single collection of these essays in print in English: *Music and Philosophy*, eds. Stephen Maddux and Robert E. Wood (Milwaukee: Marquette University Press, 2005), which reproduces eleven essays out of the dozens that Marcel published on the subject.

2. Gabriel Marcel, "The Finality of the Drama," in *The New Orpheus: Essays Toward a Christian Poetics*, ed. Nathan A. Scott, Jr. (New York: Sheed and Ward, 1964), p. 334.

3. Marcel, "The Finality of the Drama," p. 335.

4. Gabriel Marcel, "An Essay in Autobiography," in *The Philosophy of Existence*, trans. Manya Harari (Providence, RI: Cluny Media, 2018), p. 117.

That said, the plays are unmistakably philosophical, in that almost all of them feature extended philosophical discussions and debates on the part of the characters. No particular character, however, is ever a mere mouthpiece for Marcel's own views—religious, philosophical, or otherwise. It seems clear from what Marcel has written and said about his aesthetic method that his goal is to present a clash of ideas that refuses to resolve into a neat synthesis. The reader or the spectator takes the various melodies of the play and creates a harmony for them. This means that people who expect art to provide clear answers—theological or political—will be frustrated by Marcel's work. To appreciate his plays, we must be attuned to the mystery of human life, which drama deepens rather than dispels.

Thirst (*La Soif*) was written at an anxious time in Europe, a time when nationalist forces had fully taken over Germany and were threatening to take over the rest of the continent. War must have seemed increasingly inevitable—a war that was at the same time unthinkable after the devastation of the First World War. Marcel, along with many of his fellow Europeans, spent much of the 1930s in a state of acute anxiety; in his autobiography, *Awakenings*, he says that "this anxiety was much like the continuo of my existence until the war broke out."[5] He had not served in combat in the Great War, kept from the front by his unreliable health. Instead, he had worked for the

5. Gabriel Marcel, *Awakenings*, trans. Peter S. Rogers (Milwaukee: Marquette University Press, 2002), p. 131.

Red Cross, informing soldiers' families of the wounding and disappearance of their sons, brothers, fathers, and husbands. He was thus keenly aware of the effect war could have even on people who were not themselves in danger of being killed. Moreover, Marcel's adopted son, Jean-Marie, was twenty years old in 1937. Marcel must have worried that he would be taken away from him. (As it happens, Jean-Marie Marcel did serve in World War II, although he survived.) And Marcel perhaps had an even more personal reason to worry about Hitler's triumph: his mother had been Jewish, even if he himself had been raised without religion and converted to Catholicism in 1929, and so he was in danger of persecution if France were to be occupied by the Nazis. If Marcel himself worried about this possibility, however, he does not mention it in *Awakenings*. His anxiety seems to have been more global in scope.

And yet the circumstances under which Marcel wrote the play were personally less bleak. He and his family spent part of the summer of 1937 in Morgat, Brittany, where he alternated between working on *Thirst* and on *Colombyre, or the Torch of Peace*, his hysterical, pitch-black satire of interwar utopianism. "For some weeks," he writes, "it was as though a cover of clouds that weighed down on us had lifted. Thanks to the Universal Exposition of 1937, we again began absurdly to hope. After all, the worst was not sure to happen."[6] He goes so far as to wonder if his life did not peak that summer.

Whatever joy he felt at the time is scarcely manifest in *Thirst*: aside from some humor involving the outrageous medium Mademoiselle Freux and some dark satire of Madame

6. Ibid., p. 139.

Chartrain's bourgeois nihilism, the play is remarkably taut, oriented toward not one cataclysm but a whole series of them that feel unavoidable. The geopolitical cataclysm is only one of them, and perhaps the least immediate. Marcel is more concerned with Stella's mental health, with Alain's despair, with Amadée's failure and pulling-away from his family at the very moment they need him most. The overall atmosphere, as in so many of Marcel's plays, is of a hot room with the air progressively closing in. Even music, which often serves as a kind of fresh breeze in his drama, is conspicuously absent from *Thirst*, as if to suggest that the dread of the Chartrain and de Puygerland families must be suffered, gone through, rather than avoided. Whatever grace we find at the end of the play—and we do, I believe, find some hope for the future there, which is not exactly the same thing as relief—that grace comes only through these families' suffering.

The emotional weight of the play lies mainly on the shoulders of Stella, a twenty-year-old woman who is haunted by the death of her mother a few years earlier. It is not exactly, or exclusively, grief that she feels. Rather, she is worried that the mental illness which drove her mother to take her own life is hereditary and will eventually destroy her as well. Her anxiety, however, is its own kind of debilitating illness, and when she agrees to marry Alain de Puygerland, her stepmother, Eveline, worries that she is doing so not out of love but out of total despair for her future. Nearly every character in the play feels some variation of that despair. Alain is certain that France will go to war with Germany and that he will be drafted and killed. Stella's father, Amédée, having been forced out of his job, is certain that he is condemned to failure. And Eveline herself, having bound her life to Amédée's, senses that she has made a terrible mistake. The future stretches out like a no man's land for Marcel's characters, promising only pain; as such, their emotions, if not their situation, must echo the feelings of millions of Europeans of good will in 1937.

Only two Chartrains are not weighed down by this despair. Amédée's mother is marked by a blithe complacency that allows her to say that the poor and the disabled would be better off if they were euthanized, unaware of, or apathetic to, her granddaughter's concerns for her sanity. She has no fear of Hitler because she admires him and hopes that France will collaborate with his fascist government. Marcel plays her for comedy and horror, more or less at the same time. *Thirst* opens with her and Stella trying to decide how much money to give to various charity cases. The first lines of the play are Madame Chartrain's exclamation: "My eyes! My eyes!" (p. 5). But this is histrionic, just a way of saying that she needs her glasses to see well. She has no real experience of the suffering that has overwhelmed her family, not to mention that of the unfortunate people asking for her help.

Arnaud, Stella's brother, continues the trend which Marcel started with *The Sandcastle*, his second published play, of including characters who have entered, or are considering entering, religious orders. A lesser Catholic playwright would use such a character as a vehicle for the author's religious beliefs, but Marcel largely resists that temptation. Or at least we can say that Arnaud is the voice of true faith but still merely one voice among the many in the play. Other characters, particularly Stella and Eveline, occasionally envy him for the faith that allows him to navigate his own grief, anxiety, and despair—but at other times, they resent him for his tendency to stand removed from their suffering, a tendency no doubt exacerbated by his desire to enter the monastery. He tells Maggie, a young woman to whom he is clearly attracted and whom, if not for his religious vows, he might have married, that "I live at sea…and you—you prefer terra firma" (p. 155). We can understand his family's frustration with him, but the religious reader or viewer of *Thirst* will no doubt also understand Fr. Marcel Belay's reading of Arnaud:

> Faith opens our eyes to this demand of transcendence and reveals the Reality that can respond to it. It's to let himself be penetrated by the fullness of this Reality that the man dedicated to God consents to die to himself. Through this death to himself, inscribed in his vocation, Arnaud can discover the positive significance of death: the opening of an infinite charity for which we here below already have nostalgia, a nostalgia that constitutes the very essence of our existence.[7]

In some ways, we should perhaps see Arnaud as caught between two worlds, the possessor of a hope that his family desperately needs, a hope that he cannot truly communicate to them because it must be lived rather than merely spoken. This extends to the audience as well. When the critic Hilda Lazaron writes that, despite its many discussions of religion, *Thirst* "fails to be convincing regarding Marcel's religious convictions,"[8] I

7. Marcel Belay, *La Mort dans le théâtre de Gabriel Marcel* (Paris: Librairie Philosophique J. Vrin, 1980), p. 113. Translation mine.
8. Hilda Lazaron, *Gabriel Marcel the Dramatist* (London: Colin Smythe, 1978), p. 100.

wonder if it is not so much a philosophical or aesthetic failure on Marcel's part as it is a sign of the fundamental incompatibility of theological assertion with Marcel's brand of heteroglossic drama.

Still, we ought to pay special attention to Arnaud, if only because Marcel, in his last days on earth, writes that he has taken as his own Arnaud's question: "Do you never wonder what you're living on?" (p. 183).[9] When Marcel reconsidered this question, he felt that his creative, critical, and philosophical work had come to an end, and perhaps he was trying to avoid Eveline's response: "I'm like the others. I only survive on the condition that I don't wonder" (p. 183). We might conclude that Arnaud's role in the play is to keep his family—and, by extension, the audience—from falling into the ditch of easy bourgeois answers on the one side and the gaping abyss of despair on the other: to keep us walking the narrow road of wonder and reflection that sometimes leads to faith, though this destination is by no means a guarantee. "You've broken me," Eveline tells him, but he disagrees: "I think that I've removed from you something that would have suffocated us" (p. 183). Marcel's drama at its best (and *Thirst* is among his best plays) limns that suffocation and points beyond it, however tenuously and ambiguously.

As far as I can tell, there have been only two public productions of *Thirst*. In early March 1949, it was put on in Marseille

9. Marcel, *Awakenings*, pp. 235–36.

by the club de Provence au Théâtre du Gymnase; three years later, it showed at the Théâtre du Parc in Brussels.[10] This second production changed the title of the play to *Les Coeurs Avides* (*The Eager Hearts*), in order to avoid confusion with Henri Bernstein's 1949 play *La Soif*. As that play is largely unknown in English, I see no problem with returning *Thirst* (*La Soif*) to its original title. My hope is that this translation will bring Marcel's drama to a new English audience, and especially that it will lead to new productions of this play and his many others. With that in mind, I have chosen a relatively informal style for much of the dialogue—the exception being that of Amédée Chartrain, whose grandiloquence and pretention are essential parts of his character.

I am thankful to Diana Burg for her help in translating the newspaper notices at the beginning of the first act, and to Mary Meehan at the Crown College library for helping me find a French version of the play.

Michial Farmer
MARCH 25, 2021

10. Lazaron, *Gabriel Marcel the Dramatist*, p. 96.

THIRST

OR

EAGER HEARTS

To the memory of DOUSSIA ERGAZ

–G. M.

CHARACTERS

AMÉDÉE CHARTRAIN, 50

ARNAUD CHARTRAIN, 24

ALAIN DE PUYGUERLAND, 23

EVELINE CHARTRAIN, 34

STELLA CHARTRAIN, 20

MADAME CHARTRAIN, 72

MADAME DE PUYGUERLAND, 48

MADEMOISELLE FREUX, 60

MAGGIE LAMBERSART, 32

The play takes place in 1937.

ACT ONE

A large room in a country house,
about a hundred kilometers from Paris.

SCENE I

Madame Chartrain, Stella

MADAME CHARTRAIN

with agitation

My eyes! My eyes!

STELLA

peaceably, handing her her glasses

Here you are, Grandmother.

MADAME CHARTRAIN

Thank you, my child.

She has taken a moleskin notebook and a pencil off the table.

I'm listening.

STELLA

reading a bulletin

"Madame F., widowed with three children, the eldest of whom is six years old—"

MADAME CHARTRAIN

The number.

STELLA

578.

MADAME CHARTRAIN

Read that over.

STELLA

"Madame F., widowed with three children, the eldest of whom is six years old, is currently found in the most complete destitution. She's not entitled to unemployment benefits. Her husband, having been drinking—"

MADAME CHARTRAIN

But she's a widow! ... Poorly written.

STELLA

"—wasn't paying attention when a car came toward him—"

MADAME CHARTRAIN

I see. A family of alcoholics. Nothing much to hope for. Five francs.

She writes it down.

STELLA

But, Grandmother...

MADAME CHARTRAIN

The next one.

STELLA

reading

"Mademoiselle Y.—"

MADAME CHARTRAIN

Are we saying 579?

STELLA

"—deaf-mute from birth, is losing her vision."

MADAME CHARTRAIN

Interesting. Read slowly, Stella.

STELLA

"Until now, she's lived on the material help of a far-off parent who, thanks to a reversal of fortune, finds herself incapable of providing for her needs any longer. Mademoiselle Y. also suffers from rheumatoid arthritis—"

MADAME CHARTRAIN

A desperate case. We can't do anything. The biggest favor we could do for her would be to give her a little cyanide.

STELLA

Grandmother!

MADAME CHARTRAIN

The effect is immediate. We'll get there, believe me. There are still a lot of prejudices to break through.

STELLA

I don't think they're prejudices.

MADAME CHARTRAIN

You have no social sense, sweetheart. This isn't the first time that I've noticed it. Besides, you're all reactionaries here. Okay, the next one.

STELLA

reading

"Monsieur N., German Jewish refugee—"

MADAME CHARTRAIN

I gave ten francs to their committee. That would be a duplicate.

STELLA

"Madame C., widowed with three children—"

MADAME CHARTRAIN

Again!

STELLA

It's not the same woman. "—will be forced to separate from them if she's not helped."

MADAME CHARTRAIN

Too vague.

AMÉDÉE *has opened the back door and is standing there immobile.*

STELLA

reading

"They currently live in an unhealthy room, opening into a small yard. The three children sleep in the same bed."

AMÉDÉE *coughs quietly.* STELLA *turns around.*

What is it, Papa?

AMÉDÉE

after a moment

I don't like these dictations of misfortune.

He exits.

MADAME CHARTRAIN

What did your father say? I didn't hear him very well.

STELLA

embarrassed

Something about the bulletin… Grandmother, are you sure that what we're doing here serves a purpose?

MADAME CHARTRAIN

How's that?

STELLA

Sifting through them… I don't know, when I think of all these unfortunate people… I'm ashamed…

MADAME CHARTRAIN

If you let your imagination run wild, you're lost. Charity can only be done from a distance and with a clear head.

STELLA

Yes, but...maybe that's not charity anymore.

MADAME CHARTRAIN

You've got a nasty look on your face, sweetheart, you're not like you are other Wednesdays. What's wrong? Come on, Stella, you know that I don't like secrets.

STELLA

It's nothing at all, Grandmother, I assure you.

MADAME CHARTRAIN

In that case, let's continue.

SCENE II

The same, Eveline

EVELINE *picks up a few different objects. It's clear that she's looking for something that she's misplaced.*

EVELINE

I beg your pardon, Mother. Don't disturb yourself.

MADAME CHARTRAIN

acidly

How do you expect us to do any serious work when we're interrupted every second, Eveline?

EVELINE

to STELLA

My dear, you haven't seen my work, by chance? I don't know what I did with it.

STELLA

Maybe you left it in the garden last night.

EVELINE

You think so?

She sees MADAME CHARTRAIN's *exasperation.*

(*With a little laugh*) It's idiotic.

MADAME CHARTRAIN

It's annoying, to say the least. A person would think that time has no value to you, Eveline, it's strange. Yesterday, I counted, you spent eighteen minutes looking for your handkerchief, your gloves...

EVELINE

That's possible.

STELLA

May I be excused, Grandmother? ...

MADAME CHARTRAIN

sharply

Why?

STELLA

Basically...you don't need me.

MADAME CHARTRAIN

acidly

I have to ruin my eyes on that text, which is printed much too pale and too thin... You know what my oculist told me. But that doesn't matter to you... Will I at least be able to count on you to put the money orders in the mail?

EVELINE

Rosa will take care of that, Mother.

MADAME CHARTRAIN

You're not thinking, Eveline. My charity has nothing to do with maids.

She exits, furious.

SCENE III

Stella, Eveline

STELLA

Poor Grandmother!

EVELINE

Yes, it seems to me she's getting upset a lot these days.

STELLA

You talk about her like she's ill.

EVELINE

She has an extraordinary vitality, to be sure.

STELLA

That's true.

EVELINE

The vitality appropriate for certain people who have otherwise been mummified.

STELLA

Mummified?

EVELINE

The lack of a heart preserves a person marvelously, Stella, believe me. My father, for example: if not for that stupid accident, I'm convinced he would have died a centenarian.

STELLA

Did he love life?

EVELINE

Hard to say. Loving life is still a kind of generosity, it's not given to everyone. He held onto life like he held onto his books, like he held onto his paperwork... Let's not talk about him, my kitten, that'd be better.

STELLA

And your mother? You talk about her so rarely.

EVELINE

Mama was something else. She wasted herself—first for her mother, who was hellish, and then for her husband. He killed her.

STELLA

Oh!

EVELINE

Slowly, conscientiously.

STELLA

What do you mean, killed?

EVELINE

Flowers in a vase...if you carefully fail to water them...

STELLA

How horrible! … And he never had any…remorse about it?

EVELINE

He took her death as a personal insult.

STELLA

after a moment

I've often wondered what would have happened if you hadn't come to Silvaplana the year when Arnaud and I were there.

EVELINE

If I hadn't met you, Stella, I would have left. I had decided to leave. I'd looked into it, I could have gone to Vienna as an au pair. I would have given French lessons…so as not to owe anyone anything.

STELLA

You would have left your father without feeling bad about it?

EVELINE

Without feeling bad about it in the least, my dear…

STELLA

And later, you wouldn't have blamed yourself?

EVELINE

You brooding little thing![1] No blame at all.

1. Eveline says this sentence in English.

STELLA

We're not very alike.

EVELINE

Fortunately, my dear.

STELLA

For whom?

EVELINE

Maybe for you, certainly for the others.

STELLA

following her train of thought

And us—if we hadn't met you, the three of us… Look at the difficult weeks that Papa was going through at that time… Without you! … He had such a need to be understood. We were bruising him at times without suspecting it, by a simple word that we said—or didn't say.

EVELINE

sweetly

You shouldn't worry about it, believe me.

STELLA

You always know how to see what's serious and what's not important. It's like Arnaud…

EVELINE

sadly

There's a big difference between me and your brother, don't forget that.

STELLA

I know. Arnaud is lucky to be so sure, so…

EVELINE

Yes… But it's doing him a disservice to talk about his luck. A person's luck, you see, might not have happened. It could just as easily leave him.

STELLA

That's true, you can't imagine Arnaud without his faith. It wouldn't be him anymore. He wouldn't be there anymore.

EVELINE

And yet he never talks about it. He's like a man who carries a marvelous object that's only visible to him. Other people are only allowed to see the reflection in his eyes. But that's still a lot.

STELLA

When you've always lived with him, that doesn't help anymore at all…sometimes it's even annoying.

EVELINE

You're preoccupied, Stella, I felt that immediately.

A silence.

STELLA

in a choked voice

I'd rather not talk about it. Not even to you.

EVELINE

As you like, my dear.

STELLA

You understand—

She cuts off.

SCENE IV

The same, Amédée

AMÉDÉE

speaking with his eyes half-closed

I wouldn't want there to be any misunderstanding between us. (*To* STELLA) You probably told Granny what I said just now?

STELLA

What did you say, Papa?

AMÉDÉE

It's unpleasant to have to quote yourself. You should spare me the trouble.

STELLA

I assure you that I don't remember at all.

AMÉDÉE

after a silence

This has been two days in a row that they've forgotten to empty my wastepaper basket. I'd understood that you were going to take charge of that, Stella.

STELLA

There's no rule, it seems to me.

AMÉDÉE

Isn't that regrettable?

STELLA

Ah! I know now. You said that you didn't like incantations of misfortune.

AMÉDÉE

very nervous

Dictations, dictations.[2] That doesn't at all mean that I blame you for looking with pity on those wreckages of human choice...

EVELINE

Amédée!

AMÉDÉE

Well! It's probably quite natural that people who are very young or who are, alas, in decline, like my mother—

EVELINE

to STELLA

Maggie hasn't called?

STELLA

I don't think so. You were saying, Papa?

---

2. The error is hard to express in English. Amédée said *florilèges*, "anthologies." Stella misheard him as *sortilèges*, "spells."

AMÉDÉE
to EVELINE

You have a rather disconcerting habit of cutting people off, Eveline. Who is Maggie?

EVELINE

You know the answer to that question, Amédée.

AMÉDÉE

And yet I imagine that this isn't about Mademoiselle Lambersart.

EVELINE

I only know one Maggie.

AMÉDÉE

And that...person was supposed to call you?

EVELINE

Yes.

AMÉDÉE

It was agreed that she would call you?

EVELINE

Why not?

AMÉDÉE

This was something you arranged?

EVELINE

What of it?

AMÉDÉE

I sometimes find myself answering the phone, Eveline. So I've been running the risk of finding myself in the presence—

EVELINE

On the other side of a wire.

AMÉDÉE

Let's not play with words. In the presence of a person close to the man whose unusual processes have just broken my life into pieces? Eveline, do you see what almost happened?

EVELINE

You would have passed the phone to me.

AMÉDÉE

But besides that, what's even more serious is that you're still in a relationship with the daughter of my worst enemy!

EVELINE

I've already told you that there's probably a lot of misunderstanding there.

AMÉDÉE

No, Eveline, there's no misunderstanding, there's not the slightest misunderstanding.

EVELINE

You also have to know the other side of the story.

AMÉDÉE *brings his hand to his face as if someone had just slapped him.*

AMÉDÉE

So my pain, my indignation, my disgust…it's one side of the story… What I say is subject to caution. You feel the need to inquire into it, to examine it…

EVELINE

And why not? That's exactly why I'm impatient to talk to Maggie.

AMÉDÉE

Where were you supposed to meet that silly woman? Neutral terrain, I hope?

EVELINE

Why not here?

AMÉDÉE

Ah! No, Eveline, not here, not at my house, not under my roof… or else I'll give the place up—and probably for good.

STELLA

Come on, Papa, you don't have to take it all so tragically. The moment that that conversation caused you pain, I'm quite sure that Eveline would give it up voluntarily.

AMÉDÉE

My child, why do you insist on saying "Eveline"? That shocks me, do you know that? I've asked you several times to say "Mama."

STELLA

Listen, that doesn't correspond to my feelings for Eveline. It would be artificial.

AMÉDÉE

Artificial! Politeness is artificial, decency is artificial...

EVELINE

Don't insist, Amédée. Even if Stella consented to it, I don't want it. Why don't you recognize that you don't need to intervene on this point? And besides, it's puerile.

AMÉDÉE

There's a certain live-and-let-live attitude in personal relationships that I will never tolerate in my household... Ultimately, it's all very serious.

STELLA

Why, Papa?

AMÉDÉE

It's yet another sign of the decadence into which this country sinks a little more every day.

STELLA

I don't understand.

AMÉDÉE

My poor child, if instead of feeding yourself God knows what incoherent and truant books, you'd made a methodical—and intelligent—effort to understand the history of our manners, our institutions…

SCENE V

The same, Arnaud, Madame Chartrain

ARNAUD

Bonjour, everyone. I just saw Maggie, Eveline. She asked me to tell you that she'll come see you here in an hour.

AMÉDÉE *heads toward the back door.*

Why are you leaving, Papa?

AMÉDÉE

Your stepmother and your sister know what I think about this visit. I believe I expressed myself very clearly just now. But I will add, for your information, that, being aware of the events of the last few months, you were obliged to make that blockhead understand the impropriety of the step she's taking.

EVELINE

There's no question of taking any step, Amédée, you're dreaming… Maggie is my friend, and I have nothing to be mad at her about. Now, please go take a walk while she's here, I don't see anything inconvenient about that.

AMÉDÉE

A thousand thank-yous for your leniency…

MADAME CHARTRAIN appears at the back. She seems to be equipped for a far-off expedition.

MADAME CHARTRAIN

I'm going to the post office.

AMÉDÉE

to EVELINE

The consequences of your attitude could be…limitless.

EVELINE

I've never been very afraid of what's limitless, Amédée.

MADAME CHARTRAIN

I repeat that I am going to the post office myself.

ARNAUD

Nothing pressing, Grandmother, the courier won't leave before this evening.

MADAME CHARTRAIN

It's a matter of principle.

AMÉDÉE

Mama, wait for a second, will you? I'll go with you.

They exit.

SCENE VI

Eveline, Arnaud, Stella

EVELINE

gaily

No need to hide it, my children, we'll bail out.

ARNAUD

What's happened?

EVELINE

looking in the direction they left

The two of them are so much alike!

STELLA

frightened

You think so?

EVELINE

Prodigiously.

STELLA

I'd never thought so. Papa is so sensitive.

EVELINE

peaceably

Well, I think there's a difference between them…let's say a

difference of…tempo.

ARNAUD

laughing

What are you getting at?

STELLA

to EVELINE

You say…frightening things jokingly.

EVELINE

Do I seem terrified, my dear? You know me well enough now to suspect that I could never stop myself from sometimes looking at the people I'm closest to as if they were strangers, passersby.

STELLA

And the two of us—Arnaud and I—do you…

EVELINE

But of course. Passersby to whom I have an irresistible desire to cry out, "I like the two of you so much!" In my childhood, Stella, and even since then, I've known these temptations, but I've almost never been able to resist them.

STELLA

With men, too?

ARNAUD

Of course. Why not? I'm like you, Eveline, it's just that I don't try to resist it.

STELLA

For a boy…it's easier.

ARNAUD

But with everyone, with old people, young people, children. That's why I like to travel by rail.

EVELINE

I'm going to leave you with that, my children. I need to take care of the menu, it's high time. If Maggie comes, send her to my bedroom.

She exits.

SCENE VII

Arnaud, Stella

STELLA

nervous

I have so many things to tell you, to ask you, and you're never here. This morning I even got up early. That doesn't help me, when you're at the church.

ARNAUD

softly

Maybe it helps you a bit more than you think.

STELLA

I know what you mean, but if I don't feel it, you understand…

ARNAUD

I think you shouldn't ask to feel too much. That's not good for anything.

STELLA

The atmosphere here has become very heavy, you don't seem to notice it. And yet you heard what Eveline said just now. If that's where she is after eighteen months of marriage…

ARNAUD

I don't want to talk about Eveline's feelings. They don't have anything to do with us. And besides, it's quite probable that we can't understand them at all.

STELLA

You're always retreating, how convenient... Living—I find that very difficult. Do I make you pity me?

ARNAUD

No. I feel for you.

STELLA

I almost like it better when you shake me up.

ARNAUD

But when that happens, you accuse me of mistreating you.

A silence.

STELLA

lowering her voice

In a few minutes, Mademoiselle Freux is coming to see me.

ARNAUD

Who is that?

STELLA

Arnaud!

ARNAUD

Ah! Right. I'd forgotten her name.

STELLA

Where is your head?

ARNAUD

Did she write to you?

STELLA

A little note that I received last night. Here it is.

She hands him a letter.

ARNAUD

after having read it

Funny handwriting. Disguised, you'd say.

STELLA

She herself is disguised, you know that.

ARNAUD

I'm sorry that you're seeing her again.

STELLA

She wanted to chat with me. It would have been simply cowardly for me not to go along with it.

ARNAUD

I'm not sure about that.

STELLA

Why not?

ARNAUD

You think she wanted to talk to you about Mama?

STELLA

I'm certain of it.

ARNAUD

Yes, well...

STELLA

passionately

I can't understand you. We've tormented ourselves so much trying to figure out what happened...

ARNAUD

Not me.

STELLA

So you say... That incomprehensible illness they didn't want to give us any details about...and her death, Arnaud, her death... which we didn't even learn about until three weeks later... You've also been haunted by all that.

ARNAUD

I went along with you. It's like those walks that I wouldn't have taken without you, through Achicourt or the Maison-Rouge.[3]

3. Both communes in northern France.

STELLA

Arnaud! What does that have to do with it? ...

ARNAUD

I think I'm not curious.

STELLA

It's about our mother, Arnaud, not a stranger.

ARNAUD

All the same, it's a kind of...curiosity.

STELLA

Not for me...it's anguish...it's remorse. I won't be able to think of Mama the way I should, as long as I don't know what her life was.

ARNAUD

Why not?

STELLA

I don't know how to pray.

ARNAUD

I'm sorry, Stella.

A silence.

(*Softly*) It's just, you know, maybe I'm not as simple as you imagine, and I assure you...

STELLA

Yes, Arnaud, you're the simplest of men. I mean, you wouldn't even know how to lie if you wanted to. You'd confuse yourself like a little child.

SCENE VIII

the same, Maggie

MAGGIE

Bonjour, Mademoiselle. (*To* ARNAUD) Did you tell Eveline what I said?

ARNAUD

Yes, yes, she's expecting you.

STELLA

Take advantage of my father's being out. He could get back at any minute.

MAGGIE

I imagine he won't eat me if we run into each other.

STELLA

I can't disguise the fact that he was very upset…

MAGGIE

How's that?

STELLA

Me, I don't have an opinion, but he's convinced that he's been the victim of an…an intrigue.

ARNAUD

Come on, Stella.

STELLA

You know quite well that I'm not exaggerating.

EVELINE

entering

I thought I heard your voice, Maggie. How's it going? How long have you been in Orchamp?

MAGGIE

Since the night before last. But tell me, Eveline, it seems that your husband is imagining something?

EVELINE

I'll explain. There's no need to take anything tragically.

MAGGIE

inflaming

Because I, as far as Papa goes, you understand...

EVELINE

Of course, Maggie.

MAGGIE

Papa is an amazing person. So straight, so loyal...he's formidable. I don't know...he's... Well, what does your husband blame him for?

ARNAUD

My father thinks, I believe, rightly or wrongly—

STELLA

Listen, Arnaud…

ARNAUD

—that it's been made necessary for him to abandon the direction of the *Review of Letters*, all while doing him the honor of refusing his resignation.

MAGGIE

What does that mean, "necessary"? All *I* know is that your father, according to what my father says, is the most susceptible man on earth, that he makes drama out of the most insignificant events, that he never sees anything but personal insults everywhere. Papa, who is patience itself, ended up being pushed too far, and it's quite natural—

SCENE IX

the same, Amédée

AMÉDÉE

Congratulations, Mademoiselle. You've come into my house to make my faults clear to my family. That's a very delicate process, and quite worthy of the age we live in. My compliments, Mademoiselle. It's true that you went to a good school, Mademoiselle.

MAGGIE

in a fulminating voice

Monsieur, I won't allow—

EVELINE

Come now, Maggie, don't you see that all of this is a burlesque? Come walk in the garden with me, that'll be much better.

MAGGIE

Well, it's good to please you!

EVELINE

Yes, yes.

MAGGIE

It really took Papa's incredible good will, his leniency…

She exits with EVELINE.

SCENE X

Amédée, Stella, Arnaud

AMÉDÉE

That's strange... Did you notice the stigmata of degeneracy on that woman's face?

ARNAUD

simply

I don't know, I think Maggie's ravishing.

AMÉDÉE

What?

ARNAUD

I think she's not the sharpest knife in the drawer and that she has a nasty temper, but—

AMÉDÉE

Ravishing? She's prognathous!

ARNAUD

I don't know anything about that.

STELLA

What does that mean, "prognathous"?

AMÉDÉE

My poor children, I don't know what worries me more, your crass ignorance—the ignorance of an illiterate—or, what's even more serious, a kind of philistine opacity...

ARNAUD

It's not my fault if I think Maggie is ravishing.

AMÉDÉE

Assuredly. A deformed being isn't responsible for its deformity.

ARNAUD *bursts out laughing.*

What's laughable about that? Once again, I voluntarily wonder if the part that belongs to free will in our manner of being isn't much larger even than people commonly believe. (*To* ARNAUD) And besides, my child, to believe some doctor they revere in the Church that's yours and that I honor infinitely—

ARNAUD

I'm not a theologian, Papa.

AMÉDÉE

Even without being a theologian, it seems to me that you'd be interested in thinking your faith out more. Your beliefs, which it would be, as you know, so sweet for me to share, seem to me to take everything... (*To* STELLA, *who is yawning*) Stella, doesn't your digestion need to be somewhat monitored?

STELLA

Why, Papa?

AMÉDÉE

These untimely yawns…

SCENE XI

The same, Eveline

EVELINE

returning from the garden

It's starting to rain.

STELLA

Has Grandmother come back?

AMÉDÉE

Your poor grandmother is at the post office. Madame de Puyguerland, whom we ran into coming out, took her in her car and will bring her back in a few minutes.

ARNAUD

to EVELINE

And Maggie?

EVELINE

She didn't want to offend your wrath a second time, Amédée. If you think you've intimidated her, I have to tell you you're wrong. She knows herself, that's all. She knows that she has trouble controlling herself, and she was afraid…

AMÉDÉE

It doesn't matter what that person says or thinks, Eveline. But am I to understand that you've passed over to the enemy's side? That would be more serious.

A silence.

My poor children, that's a terribly significant silence, isn't that right?

EVELINE

Listen, my friend, when a question is empty of meaning, it seems to me charitable to leave it without an answer.

AMÉDÉE

suddenly

Eveline, do you realize that I've aged ten years in the last six months?

EVELINE

Who could have put that idea in your head?

AMÉDÉE

It's not an idea, Eveline, it's obvious. I shave every morning, Eveline. I see my face in the mirror.

EVELINE *is taken in a fit of mad laughter.*
ARNAUD *also laughs.*

AMÉDÉE

Leave it alone, my child. I like that laughter, it clears things up for me. I'm not talking about Arnaud. He's subject to a sort of hilarity that you find in certain people who are a bit...rudimentary.

ARNAUD

Thanks.

AMÉDÉE

But your stepmother's laughter is...painfully instructive for me.

EVELINE's *laughter redoubles.*

A man who grows old, a man who suffers, a man betrayed by his friends after having been betrayed by...life itself—that's funny, Eveline, of course, that's an irresistible bit of humor.

EVELINE

still laughing

I beg your pardon, Amédée...it's grotesque, I recognize that...I can't...

She exits hurriedly, holding her handkerchief over her mouth. A silence.

SCENE XII

Amédée, Arnaud, Stella

AMÉDÉE

pointing at the door she exited through

Who is she?

STELLA

You understand, Papa…

ARNAUD

It's mechanical, it's not important in any way.

AMÉDÉE

Who is she?

STELLA

We're all a little nervous lately…the times are so heavy, it's true…

AMÉDÉE

Nervous…the times… My child, these are poor alibis. For my part, I'm not fooled by them.

ARNAUD

I was wondering if Eveline…

AMÉDÉE

Well?

ARNAUD

It's a little embarrassing for me to say.

STELLA

But what do you mean, Arnaud?

ARNAUD

embarrassed

It seems that in cases like these, women's humor becomes a little bizarre, a little capricious…

STELLA

How's that?

AMÉDÉE

If an event of that nature were going on in this house, it would be elementary not to tear the delicate envelope of…silence, of… modesty, that voluntarily encircles it. But it turns out that these rather…incongruous conjectures don't correspond to anything.

ARNAUD

You can't know, Papa. Maybe Eveline hasn't wanted to tell you anything yet.

AMÉDÉE

in a breaking tone

Not another word on this chapter. I think I'm literally…dreaming.

A silence.

My very dear friend Marie-Estelle de Puyguerland pointed out that these days your stepmother seems to be having trouble getting used to the life—a little reclusive and very contemplative—that we have a taste for here.

STELLA

I don't like it all that much, this life, and I'd even like to ask you if there wouldn't be a way for me to go to Italy for a while in September.

AMÉDÉE

To Italy? Why Italy, Stella? What could make sense of this expensive trip?

STELLA

It's not expensive out there. And the trip, with the deals they have…

AMÉDÉE

Right now, while we have to impose all sorts of limitations on ourselves… I've just, for economic reasons, canceled my subscriptions to two art reviews that I've followed assiduously for ten years. Besides, what would you do in Italy? For a long time, I've noticed your lack of resistance in museums, in expositions. And if by chance it's the landscapes that attract you, you won't find, believe me, any more worthy of love than those that our own Île-de-France presents you on the briefest walk.

STELLA

But I'm already familiar with them…

AMÉDÉE

Do you really know how to…look, Stella? I wonder. What *is* looking? When I paid for painting lessons for you, you didn't persevere in them! You lack follow-through. Perhaps that's your most serious fault, and I'm afraid that you're not prepared for disappointments. And about that—I'd point out to you, with all the tact that I'm capable of, it's surely time for you to specify your situation with young Alain de Puyguerland.

STELLA

Papa, he's a good friend, nothing more.

AMÉDÉE

impatient

Stella, please, no more of these words that aren't worth saying. I won't tell you anything new by affirming that that great dreamy boy harbors very tender feelings for you. His attitude in your presence leaves no room for doubt, and besides, his mother confirmed it to me. It's hard for me, to be sure, to form a judgment about a young man whose reserve may be his most distinctive quality. But I find in him certain traits that I've appreciated in his mother for several…decades, oh, yes! We played twenty questions together in that Parc Monceau[4] that you don't like at all, I don't really know why. And then I believe I discern in Alain

4. A historic English-style garden in the eighth arrondissement featuring a large number of unique architectural features.

de Puyguerland that modesty, that propensity toward respect, toward deference that's so lamentably absent in the greater part of your contemporaries, my dear Arnaud. I'm not talking about you at the moment, your case is entirely particular. At any rate, Stella, I can't warn you strongly enough against a certain tendency—ought we say a temptation?—which might sometimes border on coquetry.

ARNAUD

Oh! Papa, Stella isn't a coquette. I don't think so.

AMÉDÉE

One mustn't play, even involuntarily, with feelings that are, whatever their object, what may be the highest aspect of human nature.

STELLA

But it's not my fault, if Alain—

AMÉDÉE

We'll talk about it at our leisure. Here come those ladies.

SCENE XIII

The same, Madame Chartrain, Madame de Puyguerland

MADAME CHARTRAIN

Tsk, tsk, tsk, no one comes to tell me stories. Well, *I've* seen him, Monsieur Hitler. I saw him as I see you, in Bayreuth,[5] last summer. Well, I guarantee that he has an allure, and a simplicity! … He's charming. You see immediately whom you're dealing with. And then we were almost introduced at the home of Princess Whatshername, whose niece was at my hotel. Anyway, it doesn't really matter.

MADAME DE PUYGUERLAND

frightened

Weren't you intimidated?

MADAME CHARTRAIN

Me? Why? I'm not timid. Do you know what they ought to do? Invite him to Paris for the Exposition,[6] quite simply. I'm telling

5. A city in northern Bavaria, best known as the site of the Bayreuth Festival, with its presentation of Wagner's operas. Wagner himself lived there in the 1870s and built the city's opera house. Bayreuth was an important site for German nationalism in the first half of the twentieth century, in part because of Wagner's own nationalism and anti-Semitism. Hitler attended the Festival, which is presumably where Madame Chartrain saw him.

6. The Exposition Internationale des Arts et Techniques dans la Vie Moderne was held from May to November 1937 on the Champs-de-Mars in Paris. Six countries—Canada, Germany, Great Britain, Italy, the Soviet Union, and Spain—participated alongside the French. Hitler did not want

you, the Parisians would adore him. They've made a strawman of him, it's grotesque.

MADAME DE PUYGUERLAND

But do you think he'd accept?

MADAME CHARTRAIN

Joyfully. He's a tender person, that man, you only have to look at him.

MADAME DE PUYGUERLAND

But the 30th of June[7]...

MADAME CHARTRAIN

ironically

Were you there? Did you have some sort of insider tip? For my part, what they say doesn't interest me.

MADAME DE PUYGUERLAND

But the newspapers—

MADAME CHARTRAIN

The newspapers! Do you know how a newspaper is made? No? Well, I doubt it. But to come back to our Adolf, he'd need to stay

---

Germany to participate, but the architect Albert Speer, who would later be the Nazi Minster of Armaments and War Production, won a gold medal for the Germany Pavilion, and his model of the Nuremburg Nazi party rally grounds also won a first prize.

7. Presumably Madame de Puyguerland is referring to Hitler's order, on June 30, 1937, to ransack museums looking for "degenerate" art.

for a month. And then eat with some people and others. He'd see who the brave among us were. He has no idea about that. Hey, for that matter, I'd embarrass myself! I'd say: Come on, Monsieur Hitler, you're not going to make war with us! No, come on, that's not a thing that's done. It was good in the old days, but today, with our inventions, with science...come on, come on! ...

MADAME DE PUYGUERLAND

Your Grandmother is marvelous, my dear Stella.

AMÉDÉE

My mother exhibits a vitality and, I'd add, an optimism that disconcerts us and ravishes us all at once. She's the youngest of all of us.

MADAME CHARTRAIN

Of course. That's not a novelty.

AMÉDÉE

But you, Marie-Estelle—does politics awaken some interest in you?

MADAME DE PUYGUERLAND

My poor Amédée, it's terribly mingled in our lives. When a person has a 21-year-old son...

AMÉDÉE

Certainly, certainly.

MADAME DE PUYGUERLAND

It's quite difficult to not be haunted by the thought of what could happen.

MADAME CHARTRAIN

peremptorily

Sweetheart, I'm begging you, no obsessions. Otherwise you'll end up in an asylum, and that's no fun at all—especially for your circle of acquaintances. When I lost Ernest, it's quite simple: I thought I would go mad… And then I reacted. We don't have the right to let ourselves go.

MADAME DE PUYGUERLAND

Not everyone has your resilience, my dear Madame.

MADAME CHARTRAIN

That's just because no one today knows what will power is, hear you me: Will. Pow. Er.

AMÉDÉE

And yet it seems to me that Marie-Estelle, when it came to raising that tall boy with blue eyes—actually, are they blue? No, aquamarine, rather—she knew how to give the marks of a persevering devotion, something quite close to heroism. I've held onto the memory of some childhood illness—measles or scarlet fever—where for many nights—

MADAME CHARTRAIN

It would have been better for her to take precautions. What good does it do to ruin your health at the bedside of sick people? At that point, there are people who have to take care of you. That's no idea of mine.

AMÉDÉE

A certain prodigality, reasonable or not, will always merit my admiration.

MADAME DE PUYGUERLAND

a bit maliciously

What's so charming about Amédée is that he talks exactly the way he writes—and since his letters are marvelous…

AMÉDÉE

I would hate to contradict you, Marie-Estelle, but I think, on the contrary, that I literally write as I talk. I'm a greatly spontaneous man, don't forget that.

A silence.

MADAME CHARTRAIN

Oh, Stella, there's a kind of fairy godmother who claims that she has an appointment with you.

STELLA

Ah! …

MADAME CHARTRAIN

I told her to wait in the study. I suppose she's come for a book?

STELLA

with agitation

Why didn't you tell me sooner, Grandmother?

MADAME CHARTRAIN

with an ogre's laugh

The Little Hunchbacks of Valois, something in that vein... If I had advice to give you, it's not to let yourself be cheated.

STELLA

It's not what you think.

She exits.

MADAME CHARTRAIN

In any case, bring her here. It's 11:30. I'm going to go sit in the study with my books. It's too hot in here.

MADAME DE PUYGUERLAND

Do you read a lot?

MADAME CHARTRAIN

I reread. The great authors. Voltaire, Renan.[8] Pen in hand. It's my way of praying, to myself. Hahaha!

---

8. Voltaire was an eighteenth-century philosopher best known in the English-speaking world for his satiric novel *Candide* (1759). Ernst Renan was a nineteenth-century philosopher and historian of religion, the author of *Life of Jesus* (1863). Both authors were notoriously anti-Catholic and anti-clerical; additionally, there is a serious anti-semitic undertone to *Life of Jesus*, which claims that Jesus purified himself of his Jewishness.

AMÉDÉE

And you, Marie-Estelle, I hope that you won't leave yourself fallow…

MADAME DE PUYGUERLAND

I don't read anymore at all. I have a headache. And then all these events…no one saw anything coming.

AMÉDÉE

You exaggerate, Marie-Estelle. Not everyone was fooled. When I reread certain letters that I wrote to my family in 1912—I was 25 years old then—I am shocked by my clairvoyance. One day you'll allow me to read you a few passages, for curiosity's sake.

STELLA

returning, to MADEMOISELLE FREUX, *who follows her*

This way, Mademoiselle, if you would. Let me introduce you.

AMÉDÉE

when he sees MADEMOISELLE FREUX

Ah!

STELLA

My father, my grandmother, Madame Chartrain, Madame de Puyguerland. Mademoiselle Freux. Maybe it'd be better for me to show Mademoiselle to my room?

AMÉDÉE

Not at all, not at all, I'll be back right away.

STELLA

But Papa…

MADEMOISELLE FREUX

I don't want to bother anyone.

MADAME DE PUYGUERLAND

to STELLA

Do you remember that we're counting on having you tomorrow for tea? And Arnaud, too, of course.

STELLA

But I don't know if I'll be able to…

MADAME DE PUYGUERLAND

Don't miss it, my dear. Alain would be too sad… I don't think he's well at the moment. Au revoir.

Handshakes.

AMÉDÉE

I'll show you to your car, Marie-Estelle.

MADAME CHARTRAIN

And I'll return to my *People of Israel.*[9] It's exciting. Ah! These Jews, all the same… And yet Monsieur Hitler isn't entirely wrong. Well, au revoir.

9. That is, Renan's five-volume *History of the People of Israel* (1887-1893).

Thirst

She tips her head toward Mademoiselle Freux
and exits stage right.

SCENE XIV

Stella, Arnaud, Mademoiselle Freux, then Amédée

MADEMOISELLE FREUX

planting herself in front of ARNAUD

He looks so much like his poor mama! ... I would have recognized him in the street.

ARNAUD

We've met before, Mademoiselle, it seems to me.

MADEMOISELLE FREUX

It was so long ago...

STELLA

in a trembling voice

I would have thought I'm the one who looked like my mother.

MADEMOISELLE FREUX

Something in your face...and also in the timbre of your voice. But him—he has the oval, the mouth, the chin...

STELLA

Is that true?

ARNAUD

Resemblances always seem so vague to me.

MADEMOISELLE FREUX

Crying out, I repeat it.

STELLA

Take a seat, Mademoiselle. I'm so happy you were able to come… I was afraid… Since that meeting at the Maurices'…it was so strange, so unexpected…

MADEMOISELLE FREUX

Not for me. I knew.

STELLA

How's that?

MADEMOISELLE FREUX

I'm very psychic. I have intuitions, you understand, that are never wrong.

ARNAUD

I pity you, Mademoiselle…

MADEMOISELLE FREUX

That is to say, it's a great privilege. It must be earned. There's a whole gymnastics of the soul.

STELLA

That's extraordinary.

MADEMOISELLE FREUX

Not at all. Nothing is simpler. As long as you're properly oriented.

STELLA

By what, exactly?

MADEMOISELLE FREUX

You must be initiated, that's all.

STELLA

To what?

MADEMOISELLE FREUX

If, as I hope, our relationship continues in the future, I'll loan you some books… Hindus in particular, and Americans…and I'll introduce you to some magnificent people. It's a whole world that you have no idea about.

STELLA

But in the meantime, Mademoiselle, we'd like so much…right, Arnaud? I'm counting on you, Mademoiselle, you can't know how much. No one ever talks to us about our mother. And you knew her so well, you told me that, and—

AMÉDÉE

coming back from the garden

I beg your pardon, Mademoiselle. I risk having seemed discourteous to you.

STELLA

If you need this room, we'll take Mademoiselle into my bedroom.

AMÉDÉE

Not at all. May I be permitted to ask you, Mademoiselle, to what honor we owe this unexpected visit?

MADEMOISELLE FREUX

So you never said anything to your father about our meeting at the Maurices'?

STELLA

No, I don't think so.

MADEMOISELLE FREUX

Strange.

ARNAUD

Mademoiselle, each of us has his own life, his own relationships...

MADEMOISELLE FREUX

Very well. But what happens to the family in all that?

AMÉDÉE

So I think I understand that you ran into my daughter at the house of...a third person.

STELLA

Jeanne Maurice, Papa.

AMÉDÉE

That name tells me absolutely nothing. It doesn't matter anyway, at least not for the moment. You had a conversation?

MADEMOISELLE FREUX

This child wasn't unknown to me. I was her dear mother's teacher and confidant.

AMÉDÉE *has an interrogative expression on his face.*

No, Monsieur, I'm not telling you anything you don't know. We've seen each other before, several times, in circumstances that you haven't forgotten. Besides, Monsieur, a person doesn't forget *me*. There's a sign on me, I know it.

STELLA

I'm the one, Papa, who asked Mademoiselle Freux to come see me, when I found out that she lived with friends around here. Arnaud and I have questions to ask her.

AMÉDÉE

Arnaud? … Questions? …

ARNAUD

Stella has been quite tormented lately.

STELLA

I'm begging you, Arnaud, not now… If you'd like, Mademoiselle, we'll go upstairs to my room, where we won't be disturbed.

AMÉDÉE

I won't stand for it. May I ask you, Mademoiselle, if you've attempted to correspond with my children?

MADEMOISELLE FREUX

disdainfully

Letters! ... I only believe in presence... Besides, an event, an encounter, has to ripen like a fruit.[10] That's what we learned, along with many other things, from Madame Hélène Sidney.

AMÉDÉE

Who is Madame Hélène Sidney?

MADEMOISELLE FREUX

You don't know who Madame Hélène Sidney is?

AMÉDÉE

No, Mademoiselle, I haven't the slightest idea.

ARNAUD

Me neither, I confess.

MADEMOISELLE FREUX

A man who calls himself cultivated doesn't know the existence of one of the most radiant beings who has ever appeared upon this earth—and we're astonished that poor unfortunate Europe is in chaos! How about that.

She pulls a photograph out of her purse. ARNAUD *and* STELLA *look at it over their father's shoulder.*

10. The language Mademoiselle Freux uses here is very similar to that of Marcel's essay "On the Ontological Mystery."

AMÉDÉE

Are you quite certain that's a woman, Mademoiselle? One would say a bulldog, or a clergyman.

MADEMOISELLE FREUX

I beg your pardon, Monsieur. Madame Hélène Sidney is the generator according to the spirit of Radha Murti[11]...

AMÉDÉE

Krishnamurti.[12]

MADEMOISELLE FREUX

Don't talk to me about that imposter... Of Radha Murti, the redeeming angel, the one who will snatch the world from the claws of materialism.

AMÉDÉE

Do you have her photograph, too?

MADEMOISELLE FREUX

At my house. She's playing golf.

ARNAUD *bursts into laughter.*

11. Radha is the Hindu goddess of love and beauty; *murti* is a Hindi word for *statue.*

12. Jiddu Krishnamurti (1895-1986) was an Indian teacher who was at one point associated with the Theosophical Society. He broke with the society at the end of the 1920s and spent the rest of his life as a popular teacher and speaker.

For pity's sake, don't laugh, my child. That laugh pierces the heart of your poor mama, who sees you and hears you from the depths of the great beyond…

STELLA

Papa, I'm begging you, this isn't possible, this can't go on. I feel like my head is splitting open. What harm can it do you to leave me alone with Mademoiselle Freux for a few minutes?

AMÉDÉE

On the contrary, I have the best reasons, the most peremptory reasons, not to tolerate this particular interview.

STELLA

But this is infernal. You don't have the right…

AMÉDÉE

It's not about a right here, but rather a sacred duty.

STELLA

You don't know what I want to ask Mademoiselle.

AMÉDÉE

What I really don't know is what she'd be able to say in response to your questions.

STELLA

So there's something to be afraid of?

ARNAUD

I'm begging you, Mademoiselle, don't you see that my sister is on the verge of a nervous breakdown?

MADEMOISELLE FREUX

Madame Hélène Sidney often highlighted the salutary role of shocks in spiritual development.

AMÉDÉE

That's enough, Mademoiselle. We've heard enough. You'll do me the favor of leaving this house.

MADEMOISELLE FREUX

fulminating

I'll not do anything of the sort, Monsieur. Call your butler, we'll see if he dares to lay a hand on an invalid.

SCENE XV

The same, Eveline

EVELINE

What's going on?

STELLA

Eveline, help me, Eveline…

AMÉDÉE

My dear Eveline, if you only could have come a few minutes earlier! You would have heard the most comforting assurances falling from Mademoiselle's mouth. It seems that the world is on the verge of being saved…

EVELINE

What? What?

AMÉDÉE

By a lady with the face of a bulldog and a seraph who plays golf.

ARNAUD

Eveline, take Stella away, she can't stand up any longer.

MADEMOISELLE FREUX

I'm going, I'm going… I thought about it… What new could I tell you? (*To* ARNAUD) You're an adult, I imagine? …

ARNAUD
flabbergasted
What does that have to do with anything?

MADEMOISELLE FREUX
Are you an adult?

ARNAUD
I'm 24.

MADEMOISELLE FREUX
So you've received the letter…

STELLA
What letter?

ARNAUD
What letter?

MADEMOISELLE FREUX
The posthumous letter that your mother had her notary give you when you came of age. Precisely that one.

ARNAUD
What's this invention?

MADEMOISELLE FREUX
Ask your father if it's an invention.

STELLA

Papa…

AMÉDÉE

I don't have to give an account to a madwoman.

MADEMOISELLE FREUX

Nothing would be simpler for you, my dear Stella, than to write to Monsieur Gardefeu, your mother's notary. You'll easily find his address, and his telephone number… Okay, okay, I'm leaving. I'm glad to see you're under a good influence… In fact, send me your horoscope sometime. Au revoir, everyone.

She exits.

SCENE XVI

Amédée, Eveline, Arnaud, Stella

STELLA

What is this letter? Arnaud, swear to me...

ARNAUD

Stella!

STELLA

So...it was stolen. Papa!

AMÉDÉE

I'm not going to reveal a demented accusation...

STELLA

passing her hand over her forehead

It's true, I'm insane. Eveline, I've gone insane...me too... (*To* AMÉDÉE) It's your fault. Why have you never wanted to tell us anything?

EVELINE

Calm down, my dear, I'm begging you...

STELLA

That interminable, incomprehensible illness... Mental, right? Mental? But what makes me think that? There are people who get shut up for no reason, because they're embarrassing... Don't deny it. I know what things happen. I've read about it. And the last moment that I saw her...

ARNAUD

You're wrong, my dear Stella, I swear.

STELLA

What allows you to affirm that? What have you learned?

ARNAUD

That's out of a novel.

STELLA

You're a coward, maybe an accomplice. I hate you, and your religion that accepts everything, that bears everything, that doesn't help anyone, that doesn't fight for anyone.

EVELINE

But you're being unfair, you're abominable, you're going to regret this, my dear...

STELLA

to AMÉDÉE

I demand that you tell me the truth. What happened? Why didn't we see her again?

EVELINE

to AMÉDÉE

Amédée...you don't have the right...

AMÉDÉE

Don't worry, Eveline.

STELLA
to EVELINE

And you, too, you're abandoning me…ah! It's awful… Mama! Mama! … (To AMÉDÉE) If you refuse to speak, I'm going to leave… I'm going to disappear… No one will stop me…

AMÉDÉE

Listen to me, Stella, for the last time. By this unusual, formal notice…

STELLA

No more fancy words!

AMÉDÉE

You're claiming, without suspecting it, I admit that…to charge my conscience with an evil action.

STELLA

Your conscience! If you only knew what that means to me!

AMÉDÉE

You're running the risk of taking on a very serious responsibility.

STELLA

Goodbye.

She runs to the door.

EVELINE

Stella!

She tries to hold STELLA *back, but* STELLA *manages to break loose.*

AMÉDÉE

She asked for it.

EVELINE

Arnaud! For heaven's sake!

ARNAUD

We can't stop him from talking.

AMÉDÉE

Stella, there's a novel that you read against my will a few months ago.

STELLA

I don't know what you're talking about. I'm not going to guess…

AMÉDÉE

Then I'll be as explicit as you ask me to… Following an attempted poisoning…

STELLA

What?

AMÉDÉE

Of which I was almost the victim—I was forced to demand the internment of your unfortunate mother.

STELLA

Poiso—she wanted to poison *you*?

AMÉDÉE

I had irrefutable evidence of it—and she herself admitted it… I had no other way of protecting the three of us.

A silence. STELLA *falls down into a chair, annihilated.* ARNAUD *drops to his knees, his head in his hands.*

EVELINE

going over to them, pulling them against herself

My dears…my children…my children! …

CURTAIN

ACT TWO

Same décor as the first act.

SCENE I

Amédée on the telephone, then Eveline and Alain

From the moment ALAIN *enters the room, we must recognize from* AMÉDÉE's *looks to the side that he is speaking to* ALAIN *at least as much as to his interlocutor.*

AMÉDÉE

What are you saying, Gargillier? I can't hear you very well. Contempt? Oh! Not even.

ALAIN

low, to EVELINE

But Madame, I'm afraid to disturb him.

EVELINE

Not at all, not at all. When my husband gets to turning one of his records…

ALAIN

He likes it?

EVELINE

He's always happy to have a listener.

AMÉDÉE

into the phone

They're making noise around me, Gargillier, excuse me. No, you see, those people don't even inspire me with contempt, I assure you. An unalloyed indifference. And maybe even that's saying too much. They're quite simply written off… How's that? … You should have your telephone looked at, Gargillier…written off as far as my universe is concerned.

ALAIN

sotto voce

Who is Gargillier, Madame?

EVELINE

A paralytic who's rather hard-of-hearing. He's the sort of person who's a little annoying but very convenient: He invites eloquence, and you've always got him at the end of a wire.

AMÉDÉE

One of them recently sent me his daughter…

EVELINE

Oh!

AMÉDÉE

Maybe to make certain overtures to me… I don't know anything about it, I didn't let her talk… You see, Gargillier, ultimately, there is only one thing that's entirely important. My son would tell you that it's salvation. Me, I think that it's self-agreement…a certain musical state of the soul.

ALAIN

What Monsieur Chartrain is saying sounds very beautiful to me.

EVELINE *looks at him with astonishment.*

EVELINE

sotto voce

Au revoir.

She exits.

AMÉDÉE

This is not without some melancholy. But serene, Gargillier, serene… I didn't ask for your news. (*Without waiting for a response*) Always the same, of course, but without aggravation, that's it, without aggravation. You're a stoic, Gargillier. We're cut a bit from the same cloth. It must be admitted, however, that destiny has judged it right to submit me to… What's that? The telephone wears you out? But you should have told me that sooner, my good friend… I would have kept myself from inflicting you with… I thought I was distracting you, Gargillier. You could have set me straight earlier. A thousand pardons. Rest, my good friend, rest.

He hangs up the phone.

That's incredible. (*To* ALAIN, *with an affected surprise*) Were you there the whole time, my dear Alain?

ALAIN

I beg your pardon, Madame Chartrain showed me in. I came to get some news about… Stella…

AMÉDÉE

Stella isn't sick, as far as I know…

ALAIN

She was supposed to come have tea with us yesterday; she said she wasn't feeling well… I was worried.

AMÉDÉE

Yes, yes, I remember now. A little fatigue because of the first hot weather. There's nothing you need to take tragically. (*With an indulgent smile*) Don't worry… Was she told you were here? She'll probably want to reassure you herself.

ALAIN

lively

No, no. Not now. I wouldn't want her to be upset.

AMÉDÉE

The very excess of your solicitude could only touch her to the quick.

ALAIN

Oh! I don't know.

AMÉDÉE *examines her with an indiscreet benevolence.* ALAIN *lowers his eyes.*

She's sometimes a little...bewildering, don't you think?

AMÉDÉE

No, I can't say that my children bewilder me.

ALAIN

Arnaud is different, he's always the same, you find him where you left him. Whereas Stella...you can never predict... She'll seem trusting, I could even say amicable, for the whole length of a walk, and then the next day she's cold, almost a stranger. Or else sometimes, in the course of a conversation, she suddenly changes: the minute before she was there with me. The next instant, she's somewhere else, I don't know where.

AMÉDÉE

You needn't, believe me, attach any particular importance to those caprices, those mood swings in a young woman.

ALAIN

I lose myself in suppositions... I torment myself...

AMÉDÉE

peremptory

You're wrong. I think a lot of these inconsistencies are bodily.

ALAIN

troubled

Bodily?

AMÉDÉE

Experience has shown me that women depend on their organism to a point that the rest of us can't even imagine. Eh! Yes, that's the price of everything that a person can love in these frail and charming beings. Moreover, make sure not to let them see that you've noticed it: they won't forgive you for that. They will never agree to a state of servitude that they judge, quite wrongly, to be humiliating for their *amour-propre*. And since in this case, they're quite inventive, they easily find justifications for such a mood swing, which, to tell the truth, doesn't involve any. Pretend to be fooled by it, you'll see that's the best way.

ALAIN

You understand women admirably.

AMÉDÉE

Say "woman" instead, my young friend. Despite appearances, she's strangely identical to herself. There are doubtless some exceptions. Your exquisite mother is one of them.

ALAIN

But Stella...

AMÉDÉE

Like all young women, Stella is still an almost virtual being. It will be up to you to perfect her, even to actualize her.

ALAIN

Up to *me*, Monsieur? Did you say that right: up to *me*?

AMÉDÉE

Without a doubt. Have I ever made a mystery of the affection that I bear for you and the satisfaction that I would experience to see you enter our family?

ALAIN

And yet you've never expressed it so clearly, Monsieur… But Stella herself…do you have reason to think…because she's never said anything to me…

AMÉDÉE

I didn't acknowledge it; I vowed it.[1] At her age, one is always tempted to show oneself to be a little stormy. But I have reasons to think that she expects something other than sighs, reticence, and tender allusions from you.

EVELINE *has noiselessly entered during this last reply.*

ALAIN

She can't have the slightest doubt…

AMÉDÉE

That's not enough, my dear Alain, believe me. Stella is like the others. She needs to feel attached, led, by a firm, responsible hand…

ALAIN

So, Monsieur, if you were me, you'd…

1. *Je ne l'ai pas confessée, je l'avoue.*

AMÉDÉE

Yes, my friend, I'd "burn my ships."

EVELINE

I, on the other hand, think you'd be committing an error to follow that advice.

AMÉDÉE

But Eveline, I didn't know that Alain had consulted you.

ALAIN

Why an error, Madame?

EVELINE

Stella is not well right now. She requires great care. A marriage proposal…

AMÉDÉE

Eveline!

EVELINE

Is this about something else? … risks causing her a fatal shock.

AMÉDÉE

What an exaggeration! Do you really think that Stella doesn't know about the feelings that Alain harbors for her?

EVELINE

That's not the issue.

AMÉDÉE

As for me, I esteem that, in finally expressing himself openly, our young friend would clean up a situation that appears to me to not be exempt from a certain morbidity.

EVELINE *shrugs.*

A shrug isn't a response, Eveline.

ALAIN

Madame, do you have reason to think that Stella would refuse?

EVELINE

I don't think she's in a state to take on a decision that would engage her existence at the moment. I think she'd say no for fear of getting too entangled.

AMÉDÉE

You don't have to predict her response. You're demoralizing a child who needs all his courage to face such a conversation.

EVELINE

I'd think it disloyal to hide my fears from him.

ALAIN

It's just Madame, that what you may not see… I can't bear this uncertainty any longer, it's destroying me. It sometimes seems to me that even a refusal would be better for me than this alternating hope and discouragement…

EVELINE

It's Stella that I'm asking you to think about right now. Don't put her in the position of demanding something of her that she can't give.

AMÉDÉE

The more I think about it, Eveline, the more your role right now seems strange to me.

EVELINE

A mother, or an older sister, wouldn't have any attitude other than mine.

AMÉDÉE

None of this insipidity, Eveline, I'm begging you.

ALAIN

Madame, why aren't you being totally honest?

EVELINE

How's that?

ALAIN

I feel like you're against me. But say it...

EVELINE

It's not about what *I* hope for or fear.

ALAIN

Yes, Madame, that's exactly what it's about. Stella won't decide anything without consulting you, you know that.

EVELINE

In the present circumstances… I could only dissuade her from it.

ALAIN

bitterly

I knew it, I knew it.

AMÉDÉE

But come now, Eveline…

EVELINE

"I think I'm dreaming." Yes, I know.

ALAIN

his voice trembling

Can I hope to learn the reason for this hostility?

EVELINE

My poor Alain, you're not thinking about what you're saying. I don't think you could give Stella the happiness—

AMÉDÉE

lifting his arms to the heavens

Happiness! One of those grand words that doesn't mean anything.

EVELINE

I don't agree, Amédée.

ALAIN

At any rate, Madame, what makes you say that I'm not capable of making her happy?

EVELINE

I'm not saying that. But I think Stella's a fragile person, who needs to be supported, helped, protected.

ALAIN

Agreed. Monsieur Chartrain himself just now—

EVELINE

And I think that you, Alain, would be interested in marrying a more vigorous young woman, or at least a more stable one, more... balanced, if you will.

ALAIN

You have a lot of contempt for both of us.

EVELINE

Not in the slightest, I swear.

ALAIN

Pity, perhaps? That's not any better. No, no, Madame, don't protest. I understand very well, I assure you. It's just that there's something that you don't understand... You see, I'm like a lot of my friends, I know the fate that's awaiting me. I know that I'll be killed very shortly. Besides, it was predicted of me... Oh! Don't smile. Well, I'm not showing off. I admit that it's a very difficult thought to bear, when a person has no faith. Very, very difficult... So, you understand, if I can't get the only thing that matters to me...it's not worth trying to live. I'd rather end things immediately—that would be deliverance.

EVELINE

My dear Alain, that's a kind of blackmail.

ALAIN

If you like. I'm not afraid of words. Not at all. If you think that my mother hasn't been blackmailing me since I was very young… So it seems very normal to me. That's all I had to say to you.

EVELINE

I hope, at least, that you won't have the…unpardonable weakness to use that weapon with Stella.

ALAIN

Why not? … If I don't have a better one.

EVELINE

Well! You're proving to me how right I am to think that this marriage would be a great unhappiness.

ALAIN

It's life, Madame, that's an unhappiness… Au revoir, Monsieur.

AMÉDÉE

Come now, come now, my friend…

ALAIN

on the verge of tears

No, no, don't stop me.

He exits.

SCENE II

Eveline, Amédée

AMÉDÉE

How moving!

EVELINE
calmly

Well, I think he's abject.

A silence.

AMÉDÉE

I'm still trying to find an explanation for such an inhumane insensitivity.

EVELINE

Oh, please!

AMÉDÉE

I'm afraid, to tell the truth, of having discovered it.

EVELINE

Oh, yes?

AMÉDÉE

The animosity that you've displayed to my dear friend Marie-Estelle, you're now transferring to her son. It's very logical.

A silence.

You're not even bothering to deny it.

EVELINE

What good would it do? It gives you so much pleasure. Savor it, my dear Amédée, savor it.

AMÉDÉE

What?

EVELINE

The sweetness of believing that I'm jealous, wicked, vile... Everyone has his little treats. Why would I bother trying to disabuse you? It would be too tedious, too difficult—and really, not very charitable. You've discovered a comfortable little conviction there that you're keeping warm...

AMÉDÉE

Only you'll find it natural for me to clear Stella up about the quality of a solicitude—

EVELINE

I advise you to be careful as far as that's concerned.

AMÉDÉE

The terrifying revelation that I was forced to make to her—

EVELINE

Now you're talking.

AMÉDÉE

—nipped in the bud whatever absurd and vague suspicion that she might have maintained toward me, and that I believe you, moreover, quite capable of trying to awaken in her.

EVELINE

No.

AMÉDÉE

It's certain that she's ready now to take full account of the admonitions that I'm going to be led to give her.

EVELINE

Against me?

AMÉDÉE

That depends entirely on your attitude. If you don't try to influence her…

EVELINE

That's my duty. I won't forsake it. Can you tell me, Amédée, where this extraordinary partiality in favor of a little neuropath comes from? I know, he's the son of an exquisite woman, who's always paid you the tenderest respect. But you declared just now that Stella needed a strong, responsible hand. After what we've just heard, can you believe for a second that that boy has the will, the self-control...

AMÉDÉE

This is a mock trial. I'm not following you down this road.

EVELINE

How convenient.

AMÉDÉE

You're too much a stranger to the life of the passions, my dear Eveline, to imagine the trouble into which they can throw a soul even a little inclined to romanticism.

EVELINE

I only know one thing: whether or not Stella's maternal heredity—

AMÉDÉE

None of that scientific jargon, I beg you.

EVELINE

—involves a real danger to her reason, it's impossible for her not to be obsessed with the fear of one day succumbing to that fatality, perhaps an imaginary fatality. In those conditions, we have an absolute duty to protect her against everything that could weaken...I don't know...her interior resistance.

AMÉDÉE

You're talking like one of those droll beings they call psychiatrists.

EVELINE

You're hiding, and I understand that. I defy you to make a single worthwhile argument.

AMÉDÉE

You don't know me very well if you haven't yet noticed that I am horrified by hair-splitting. I prefer to rely on a certain inner light. I've had no reason to repent—at least until now, it seems to me—for having listened to my familiar daemon, of preferring it to the warnings of…experts. You have everything it takes to be an expert, my dear Eveline: apparent rigor, obstinance, and, let me tell you, perhaps also a certain interior opacity. On the contrary, it seems that I have antennae. The word is a laughing matter, perhaps, but the thing itself…

EVELINE

I don't see how you've ever provided any proof of this marvelous clairvoyance. It must have come to you at a late date… Yes, your first marriage—

AMÉDÉE

I believe I told you once and for all that that subject should be crossed out from our conversations.

EVELINE

Oh! Your memory is mistaken there, Amédée. In the first days of our marriage…

She laughs.

I can assure you that you missed no occasion to introduce me to your thoughts about that forbidden domain. You even had me ask you questions—and it's only because I didn't accept your confidences as completely as you'd hoped…yes, because you felt me less disposed to pity you than your…victim, yes, I'm sticking with that, your victim…

AMÉDÉE

It seems to me that that might be enough, Eveline. Here comes my mother. No one could be more qualified to decide between us.

SCENE III

The same, Madame Chartrain

MADAME CHARTRAIN

What? What? What's going on?

EVELINE

Nothing important.

AMÉDÉE

I doubt, Mama, that you agree. So judge for yourself.

MADAME CHARTRAIN

enticed

I don't really like to put my finger between the tree and the bark. But let's see.

EVELINE

I'm not disposed to care about your opinion.

AMÉDÉE

So you recognize that my mother will say I'm right.

EVELINE

I'm sure of it.

MADAME CHARTRAIN

So?

AMÉDÉE

I will surprise you by telling you that young Alain de Puyguerland—

MADAME CHARTRAIN

What! He's in love with Stella. When she's there, he makes googly eyes at her. So what?

AMÉDÉE

Just now, Eveline was strangely obstinate in discouraging that poor child.

MADAME CHARTRAIN

What a funny idea! What did he do to you, Eveline? Hmm? … I have to say that he sometimes gets on my nerves with his frowny faces, and I wish he hadn't turned down that position at the Inspection des Finances. But with his mother's connections, he won't have trouble finding a plum job in a bank. (*To* AMÉDÉE) Well! What?

AMÉDÉE

with a little nauseated smile

You sometimes have such surprising images, Mama!

MADAME CHARTRAIN

What image? … Ultimately, he's not got a bad personality, he has money, good prospects…and then, between us, you have to see things as they are, it's not about making them difficult.

EVELINE

What do you mean?

MADAME CHARTRAIN

Come on, come on, you understand perfectly well that everyone knows her mother was institutionalized. Draw out the consequences.

AMÉDÉE

My mother, with her realistic view of the situation, is, I believe, all too correct.

EVELINE

You've already resigned yourself to marrying your daughter off at a discount price.

AMÉDÉE

Excuse me: Marie-Estelle's son—

EVELINE

A long time ago!

AMÉDÉE

You can see, Mother, that Eveline, in this situation, has lost all her sangfroid.

MADAME CHARTRAIN

I wonder why.

She laughs.

Ultimately, what can all of that do to you?

EVELINE

You don't understand what I feel for Stella. I'm not going to let her ruin her life. There's already been enough suffering in this house.

MADAME CHARTRAIN

Where did you get that, Eveline? We've always led a very pleasant life.

EVELINE

When I talk about suffering, it's obviously not you I'm talking about.

AMÉDÉE

You'll appreciate the intention.

MADAME CHARTRAIN

Moral suffering, sweetheart—in my day, we didn't make a meal of it, any more than of toothaches or renal colic. And we were right. Besides, as you're no more a Christian than I am, I don't see—

EVELINE

I hope not to be entirely insensitive.

AMÉDÉE

You're on the road, Eveline, I can't hide that from you. The rather indiscreet tenderness that you're affecting for my daughter is only made of spite for me and, I'm afraid, for you, Mama.

EVELINE

Spite! You're lending me your own feelings. I—

AMÉDÉE

Is this a declaration of war?

EVELINE

If that's what you want.

AMÉDÉE

Very well. I've always loved clear situations.

MADAME CHARTRAIN

Yes, but I like my tranquility. If you take on a certain tone, Eveline, I'm going to a hotel. At your expense, of course.

She laughs.

EVELINE

her voice trembling, to ARNAUD, *who enters at this moment*

Arnaud, will you come to the garden with me for a few minutes? I have to talk to you.

ARNAUD

Stella hasn't come downstairs yet?

AMÉDÉE

Not that I know of.

MADAME CHARTRAIN
A little girl who listens more than she should.

ARNAUD *exits with* EVELINE.

SCENE IV

Amédée, Madame Chartrain

AMÉDÉE *looks in the direction that* EVELINE *has just exited. He's taken with a sort of shiver of questionable spontaneity. His mother not paying any attention to him, he highlights it with a perceptible murmur, then by the artificial cough of a great illness.*

MADAME CHARTRAIN

drily

What's wrong with you? Are you sick?

AMÉDÉE

Not physically.

MADAME CHARTRAIN

So everything is going well. Your wife has become impossible to live with, I wonder how it'll all end.

AMÉDÉE

"A little patience, and everything will end poorly," said a humorist.[2]

MADAME CHARTRAIN

A charming philosophy. He must suffer from a stomachache,

2. The phrase is usually attributed to the Roman poet Catullus (84–54 B.C.).

your humorist. Me, I think that things usually work out pretty well—as long as you don't lose your direction.

AMÉDÉE

What do you mean by that, Mama?

MADAME CHARTRAIN

It's quite simple. A taste for pleasure. Me, I don't wake up without first saying: My dear Amélie, what will you be able to do today that will give you pleasure? I always find something. The day when I don't find it, there'll be nothing left for me but to hurry off *ad patres* by the swiftest means. Haha...

AMÉDÉE

Don't you think, though, that the thought of other people—

MADAME CHARTRAIN

Dangerous. Of course, you can't stop yourself from thinking of other people. But you shouldn't try to make them happy despite themselves. And you especially shouldn't try to put yourself in their place. For one thing, it's not possible, it's not natural. For my part, in life, I'm in favor of assigned seats. Hey, your Eveline, she hasn't understood that yet, and that's what makes her unbearable. Besides, when you know that she wanted to be a social worker...a taste for interference, nothing else.

AMÉDÉE

If I shared your views, Mama, there'd be nothing left for me, I think, except packing my bags. I don't know that "pleasure" still occupies any place whatsoever in my...ravaged existence.

MADAME CHARTRAIN

Tsk, tsk, tsk, not so ravaged as that.

AMÉDÉE

I am very alone, Mama.

MADAME CHARTRAIN

You? You've always got a little gallery with you. You only live for that. Oh! I'm not worried at all, you'll keep her until your thirst is quenched. You don't need to take me for an idiot.

AMÉDÉE

after a moment

I'm even more alone than I thought, Mama.

SCENE V

The same, Stella

She is extremely pale. She has the drawn features of someone who hasn't slept.

AMÉDÉE

with a theatrical solicitude

Have you been able to "rest" a little?

STELLA *shakes her head.*

I wonder if there isn't justification to give you a light sedative tonight.

MADAME CHARTRAIN

Ugh! All those drugs intoxicate you. She needs to take a little jog after dinner, that's all.

AMÉDÉE

with a pathetic vibrato

The poor child can't stand on her legs.

MADAME CHARTRAIN

Do whatever you can to annoy me!

She exits.

SCENE VI

Stella, Amédée

STELLA collapses into an armchair. She looks into the void.

AMÉDÉE

I notice, my poor baby—oh! without surprise—that you still haven't gotten control of yourself. I wish I'd been allowed to spare you…

STELLA

Listen, Papa, I'd like to ask you something… I recognize that it doesn't seem very nice…but you have a way of expressing yourself…right now I can't… If you wanted to make an effort to speak more simply. I'm too unhappy, too lost, you understand…

AMÉDÉE

indulgently

Yes, my child, you're very worn out… I'll contain myself, of course, I don't understand…

STELLA

Thank you.

A silence.

The letter Mademoiselle Freux was talking about, are you entirely sure? … I wouldn't have the courage anymore to read it, anyway… But I need to be able to…situate myself…

AMÉDÉE

You mustn't think of it.

STELLA

Why not?

AMÉDÉE

Your mother…lived in a world that was entirely foreign to ours. Unthinkable.

STELLA

From the beginning? … When you married her, though…

AMÉDÉE

My child… I'd much prefer to see you face the future. Your future. That shadowy past that you can't enter can only blow some kind of…deleterious vapors in your face.

STELLA

Papa, remember what you promised me.

AMÉDÉE

acidly

All the same, I can't express myself in broken English,[3] Stella.

---

3. *Je ne peux pas tout de même pas m'exprimer en petit nègre.*

STELLA

You're asking me to turn toward the future. I feel like I don't have a future. All I have in front of me is a wall. And it's precisely... the past.

AMÉDÉE

That past doesn't belong to you.

STELLA

But I belong to it. Until our vacation in Engadin[4]...

AMÉDÉE

Well?

STELLA

Until we met Eveline... Mama was part of all my thoughts, I... dedicated them to her. And then afterwards: there were two of them, that's all, or rather... Eveline, I was sure that it was Mama who sent her to me. I felt like I was being protected... I think I can't live if I don't have the feeling that someone is watching over me. Not God. I'm not like Arnaud. A real person... That's why I've always asked so few questions. I was afraid... I didn't know exactly what I was afraid of, but I was afraid. And lately the fear has grown. Until the day... And now it seems to me that I was the victim of a horrible betrayal. What may be the most awful thing is that it wasn't committed by anyone... No, I suppose that I have no one to accuse. Right? ... It's just, it's as if I were sliding away. I'm trying to hold onto myself, I can't, there's no handhold.

4. A valley in the Swiss alps.

A silence.

Why aren't you answering?

AMÉDÉE

My child, you and I are ravaged, I said that just now to your grandmother, who is too old, I'm afraid, to really get through to… Stella, we're strangely alike.

STELLA

Is that true? I wouldn't have believed it. Eveline says that you're like grandmother.

AMÉDÉE

What an aberration! You and I, Stella, we're among those very rare, painfully predestined beings who only live by their hearts… Oh, yes, my child, I'm showing you my deepest self now. By the heart alone.

STELLA

I would have thought that for you, it was intelligence, culture…

AMÉDÉE

All of that is just straw, or dry leaves. The heart, Stella, the heart![5]…

STELLA

You must have suffered so much.

5. Marcel's stage direction here has Amédée pronouncing the word *coeur* as *khoeur*.

AMÉDÉE responds only with a deep sigh.

(*Lower*) Her too?

AMÉDÉE

She belonged to another species, with which we have nothing in common.

STELLA

When...did you realize that?

AMÉDÉE

When I married her, Stella, I had no illusions. I always had the sad privilege of seeing it without trying to stop it.

STELLA

Why didn't you try?

AMÉDÉE

Amor fati. Do you know what those words mean?

STELLA

No.

AMÉDÉE

That's too bad. There's an ignorance that looks like incuriosity, like misbehavior.

STELLA

I'm sorry...

AMÉDÉE

It doesn't matter... My dear Stella, I'd like to make a sort of alliance with you.

STELLA

Why? Against whom?

AMÉDÉE

Against no one...or rather, yes: against that faceless God that we can't even incriminate and whose marionettes so many people around us are—so many people!

STELLA

I don't know whom you're talking about.

AMÉDÉE

Think, though, my dear child, about all those people who are destined to join us. I'm thinking in particular of our dear friend de Puyguerland, in whom you could find the opportunity to find tender comfort.

STELLA

Oh! Papa! ...

AMÉDÉE

I'm also thinking of someone very close to him. Is there a need to give a name?

STELLA

This is completely useless... Tell me: Do they know this horrible thing?

AMÉDÉE

I myself told Marie-Estelle about it long ago.

STELLA

You shouldn't have.

AMÉDÉE

At certain dark hours, she was my only appeal… Did she judge it right to confide that secret to Alain? It's possible. I wouldn't be offended. There's an intimacy between them that has always seemed ravishing to me.

STELLA

So he knows?

AMÉDÉE

That's quite probable…

STELLA *hides her head in her hands.*

Has knowing that in any way altered his feelings for you?

STELLA

What does that have to do with anything?

AMÉDÉE

There's no need to hide it from you. A lot of young men would turn away in a certain horror from someone…

STELLA

Ah? … Why?

AMÉDÉE

Stella, can't you guess it?

STELLA

If you wanted to be clearer…

AMÉDÉE

I'd prefer not to.

STELLA

Is it because the children of a…demented person could lose their own minds?

AMÉDÉE

At the very least, there's a very tenacious, very deep-rooted prejudice there. The fact that Alain is resolutely braving it pleads in favor of his love. Yes, Stella, that's a word that is necessary to hear without trembling.

STELLA

You say a prejudice. Why?

AMÉDÉE

It can't be about something else.

STELLA

Are you sure about that?

AMÉDÉE

It would be extremely perilous to doubt it. To believe in such a menace is to aggravate it.

STELLA

Does it exist?

AMÉDÉE

Let's beware of the faceless God.

STELLA

with disgust

Ah! … sleep…if I could only sleep.

AMÉDÉE

Without letting your grandmother know, I'll bring a pill to your room tonight.

STELLA

passionately

Do you love me a little, Papa? I'm not asking you for any fancy phrase… When you say certain words, it's as if something, I don't know, invincible, deforms them as you speak: "That's not true, that's not true, that's not true," like the beating of a pendulum. Maybe it's not your fault. Yes, maybe it's…a kind of infirmity. But what do you feel? I'm so afraid of being unfair…it would be so horrible if I misunderstood you simply because…

AMÉDÉE *puts his hand in* STELLA'S. *A silence.*

Thank you, Papa. Thank you for your silence. Yes, I feel like you were right: We're allied, but against what? Against what? Continue not to answer… (*Low*) Maybe I'm hearing…your soul…for the first time… Don't say anything, don't say anything, I'm going to close my eyes.

She stretches out on the divan, her face turned toward the wall.

AMÉDÉE

You little…magician!

A sort of jolt from STELLA *betrays the painful impression that this false note awakens in her.* AMÉDÉE *creeps off on his tiptoes. He noiselessly opens the door. It stays half-open for a moment. We hear another voice.*

Thank you.

He comes back toward STELLA*; he's holding a letter in his hand.*

Here's a letter that they just brought for you. From Alain de Puyguerland. (*With an excessive indiscretion*) I'm putting it right here. On this little table. You'll read it with a clear head.

He exits.

SCENE VII

Stella, then Arnaud

STELLA *remains motionless at first. Then she seems to want to turn over on the divan—to resume her initial position. We feel she is being worked over by an inquietude. She agitates. Finally, she gets up with a sudden movement, takes the letter, opens it with a convulsive gesture and sits down to read it. She shakes her head while she reads it. She puts the letter down next to her after having read it and is absorbed in her thoughts, her head in her hands.* ARNAUD *enters at this moment and stops, seized.*

STELLA

seeing him

Ah! You scared me…

ARNAUD

tenderly

How are you feeling now, Stel? You're still quite pale.

STELLA

Where's Eveline?

ARNAUD

I just left her.

STELLA

I know. From my bedroom, I saw you together in the garden. She was speaking animatedly...what could she have been telling you with such vehemence? ... And you, you seemed embarrassed, troubled, hesitant.

ARNAUD

gaily

You stayed at the window to spy on us?

STELLA

I was astonished...

The telephone rings.

ARNAUD

I'll go get it.

He picks up the receiver.

Hello! Is that you, Maggie? No, Eveline isn't here, but in fact, I think she's on the way to come see you... Not at all... Au revoir, Maggie.

He hangs up.

STELLA

Don't you think that she went to Maggie just to contradict Papa?

ARNAUD

Maggie is the one who came to Orchamp, I'll remind you…

STELLA

Besides, *you* are so partial to her…

ARNAUD

How's that?

STELLA

You said that you find Maggie ravishing.

ARNAUD

So what?

STELLA

She has bug eyes and a fish's mouth… But I know you've never looked at a woman in your life. Not even Eveline.

ARNAUD

All the same…

STELLA

The proof: what color is her hair?

ARNAUD

Rather…brown, it seems to me.

STELLA

Absolutely, no. Auburn. Eveline has auburn hair.

ARNAUD

If you're enjoying this...

A silence. He examines STELLA.

STELLA

You're indiscreet, Arnaud. And much too soft. When we were children, you sometimes got angry. That never happens anymore. It's a kind of senility.

ARNAUD

smiling

Go on. (*Designating the letter*) Is it that letter that's put you in the...disruptive state I've found you in?

STELLA

It causes me great joy. From now on, we're officially engaged. I'm very happy.

ARNAUD

But your eyes are full of tears.

STELLA

What does that mean—tears? You can cry out of joy.

ARNAUD

Sure.

STELLA

What do you have against him?

ARNAUD's *expression is interrogative.*

Alain, I mean.

ARNAUD

Nothing, of course. I like him a lot.

STELLA

You like everyone. A Christian way to say that you don't care about any of them.

ARNAUD

with an affectionate irony

Right. I don't care about you, for example.

STELLA

You think you're joking. But I know perfectly well that it's the truth. If you got an idea in your head, I'd lie down on the road, and you'd walk on me—oh! blessing me for it.

ARNAUD

disturbed

What idea?

STELLA

Any. A project of marriage.

ARNAUD

Now I'm reassured.

STELLA

You're not going to get married?

ARNAUD

Probably not.

STELLA

Why not? That's idiotic.

ARNAUD

Let's talk about Alain instead. Have you thought about it?

STELLA

There are opportunities. I've had time, you know. He didn't take me by surprise.

ARNAUD

No, but I'm a little surprised.

STELLA

Why?

ARNAUD

A few days ago, I would have thought that he annoyed you.

STELLA

You don't need to find someone amusing to marry him.

ARNAUD

You told me: He's spineless, he has no spirit, he's not virile.

STELLA

I really think he'd be very unhappy if I said no.

ARNAUD

Is that a good enough reason to say yes?

A silence.

STELLA

Eveline didn't indoctrinate you, did she?

ARNAUD

What?

STELLA

Just now, in the garden...

ARNAUD

Admit that you've changed your mind very suddenly, Stel.

STELLA

That's possible.

ARNAUD

Why?

STELLA

Do you think that nothing...surprising has taken place the last two days?

ARNAUD

I don't see the relationship.

STELLA

And then you—you knew. Right?

ARNAUD

after a hesitation

Yes.

STELLA

Who...told you?

ARNAUD

Papa said a few words to me...not long ago.

STELLA

And they left *me* in ignorance. Why? And when I asked you questions, you acted like you didn't know any more than I did... Oh! Arnaud, you lied to me! And that letter the old bat talked about...what is there to tell me that you didn't receive it, read it, tear it up?

ARNAUD

I swear I didn't. To acquit my conscience, I called the notary. That letter never existed.

STELLA

I have no reason to believe you. Your religion authorizes the charitable lie. Charitable! What a horrible word! Humiliating.

Humiliating. Why did they handle me with kid gloves? What were they afraid of? Didn't I have the same rights? Was it your spiritual director who recommended it? Or Eveline... Eveline... what role did she play in all this?

ARNAUD

You have no right to suspect her. She loves you with all her heart.

STELLA

You're looking at me, you're behind bars. Why don't you see that you're driving me crazy?

ARNAUD

with growing anguish

I don't want you to shut yourself up inside that idea. My dear Stel, it's destroying you.

STELLA

What are you doing to snatch it away?

ARNAUD

If you'd consent to come...to Mass sometime.

STELLA

Exactly what not to say. A drug. A preventative. What you're offering me... *Alain* loves me. Quite simply. He's offering me his hand. He's not afraid. If anyone can save me, it must be him. I'm calling him. You can listen to what I'm going to tell him.

ARNAUD

No, no…

STELLA

You're not going to stop me…

She picks up the telephone.

Number fifteen, please.

ARNAUD

Stella, listen to me.

STELLA

into the telephone

Is that you, Madame? Can Alain come to the phone? … He's gone out? Oh! … But when he comes back, if he could call me, okay? … Yes, I have something important to tell him. You're doing well? … (*In a trembling voice*) I'll come say hello at the end of the day.

She hangs up.

SCENE VIII

The same, Eveline

EVELINE

Who were you calling?

STELLA

drily

I thought you were at Maggie's.

EVELINE

No.

STELLA

Arnaud's the one who told me. She called, she's expecting you.

EVELINE

Arnaud told you about…our conversation?

STELLA

No.

ARNAUD

to EVELINE

Stella has just received a letter from Alain…

STELLA

You can say a marriage proposal. That I'm accepting.

A silence.

EVELINE

quietly, sorrowfully

What have I done to you?

STELLA

What? I don't understand your question.

EVELINE

The tone, my dear, in which you refuse to answer.

STELLA

I'm very tired. I haven't slept. You know that perfectly well.

EVELINE

Arnaud, can't you explain it to me? …

STELLA

Not in my presence.

EVELINE

Ah! You recognize…

STELLA

From this evening on, everything will be very simple. (*Suddenly*) Can I know why you've taught this lesson to Arnaud?

ARNAUD

You're absurd.

STELLA

Why this detour?

EVELINE

You've been avoiding me for two days.

STELLA

I was in bed.

EVELINE

It's as if something had severed between us—without any reason. Broken. This senseless decision…yes, I stand by that word, senseless, you've taken it against me. If I approved, you'd change your mind.

ARNAUD

I think you're mistaken, Eveline. Stella, since she found out…she imagines that there's a threat in her, a fatality, you understand. She believes she's already been rejected from the communion of human beings, excluded… Alain is offering her a refuge against other people's contempt…against her own worry…she's rushing to him.

STELLA

Enough.

EVELINE

I guessed that. But it's that very thought that you have to suffocate. Listen to me, my dear. I've often observed you with Alain. He bores you, he wears you out. He will always bore you and wear you out. I'm sure of that, I know it. He's one of those people who spend their lives pitying themselves and trying to get other people to have compassion on them. This security that you're asking him for, he's not going to give it to you. On the contrary, he'll only be able to deliver you over to those unknown powers that are in you as they're in all of us. All of us, Stella, nothing else. And precisely by trying to escape them, you're abandoning yourself to them…

STELLA

This is much too complicated for me.

EVELINE

I'm desperate.

STELLA

But what's this stubbornness about? … Why not recognize it's my father you're fighting against right now? You only have one idea, and that's to strike him, to wound him, to crush him… I've never known a less generous person.

ARNAUD

Stella!

A silence.

EVELINE

I swear you're wrong… For one thing, I don't think that he's taken this project to heart as much as you think… He has other preoccupations.

Stella makes a movement.

No. I know that you're at the decisive moment of your life, that's all.

STELLA

That's not even true. An unfortunate marriage can be undone. I have two friends who got a divorce after six months.

EVELINE

I know them. They're wrecks. Besides, you'll say anything, my dear… Do you happen to imagine that Alain will let you go? He'd cling to you… It would be hell. Stella, awful things have happened here. I don't want them to begin again. I won't allow it.

STELLA

What rights do you have?

EVELINE

Tenderness has every right.

STELLA

Tenderness! You're a hard woman, Eveline. I've seen that for a long time.

EVELINE

The thought of your happiness has never left me. I don't believe in anything but happiness, Stella. I don't trust people who deny it. It's terribly convenient, it allows for everything.

STELLA

to ARNAUD

She's still aiming at him right now.

EVELINE

Stella, for two days, you've told yourself that your father is a victim. You've fed on that conviction. That's why you're looking at me with those cruel eyes. Well, it's not true.

STELLA

I forbid you to accuse him. Arnaud, help me!

ARNAUD

Eveline, that's all so awful. Don't you see that in trying to rescue her...

EVELINE

You don't want to understand that she's being gnawed on by an error.

STELLA

No.

EVELINE

An error that's poisoning her...that's going to consume her. I swear, there's no curse on you.

STELLA

What do you mean?

EVELINE

Your mother wasn't what you think. She wasn't sick…

STELLA

So she was a criminal?

EVELINE

Not that, either.

STELLA

She wanted to kill him.

EVELINE

She wanted to live…that's all.

STELLA *lets out a cry and falls into* ARNAUD's *arms, without realizing it.*

CURTAIN

ACT THREE

Same décor. 8:30 p.m.

SCENE I

Arnaud, Madame Chartrain, in traveling clothes

MADAME CHARTRAIN

Did Aunt Mathilde come to the phone herself?

ARNAUD

Yes, Grandmother.

MADAME CHARTRAIN

But are you sure she really heard you? Her hearing has declined a lot, though she won't admit it. Did she seem surprised?

ARNAUD

Not particularly.

MADAME CHARTRAIN

So she didn't understand what you were saying. You'll have to call her back. You'd see me showing up at her house at 11 p.m. without anyone being ready to receive me! That'd be nice.

ARNAUD

You're worrying for no reason, Grandmother. I'm quite sure she's expecting you.

MADAME CHARTRAIN

You're sure, you're sure! What exactly did she tell you?

ARNAUD

I don't remember the exact words.

MADAME CHARTRAIN

furious

My dear boy, I remember how you work. You have a way of doing what people tell you to…

ARNAUD *doesn't react.*

You make my head explode!

SCENE II

The same, Amédée

AMÉDÉE

Well, I see you're already ready to pull the trigger, Mama.

MADAME CHARTRAIN

Mathilde didn't understand anything. I'll find her in bed, the maid too. I'll have no other option than to go spend the night in a hotel.

AMÉDÉE

No, no, Mama. You're tormenting yourself for no reason, I'm sure of that. Aunt Mathilde will welcome you with open arms.

MADAME CHARTRAIN

sneeringly

With her arthritis... And I'll have to submit to her jeremiads night and day...that'll be funny.

AMÉDÉE

Everyone here regrets that you've decided to leave us... Reconsider your decision again, Mama, I beg you.

MADAME CHARTRAIN

I'm not a weathervane.

AMÉDÉE

Although I do admit that a change of air would be good for you. I'm not perfectly satisfied with the way you look.

MADAME CHARTRAIN

Is that why you're sending me to Rue de Miromesnil?[1]

AMÉDÉE

No doubt Princess Tecchi won't invite you to Viareggio like last year.[2]

MADAME CHARTRAIN

Thank you. She's senile. She drools. And this car won't show up!

AMÉDÉE

It won't be long. (*To* ARNAUD) Did you call the Landrys?

MADAME CHARTRAIN

Ugh! No one understands what that boy says. With his mania for mumbling Paternosters, he's lost the habit of speaking distinctly. If I miss my train, that'll be the icing on the cake.

AMÉDÉE

You'll come back and sleep here, Mama. It won't be a great misfortune.

MADAME CHARTRAIN

Not at all. I won't be made an ass of.

1. A street in the eighth arrondissement.
2. Viareggio is a city in Tuscany, known in the twentieth century as a beach resort town and for one of the most famous carnivals in Europe. Princess Tecchi appears to be Marcel's invention.

A silence.

Stella won't deign to come say goodbye to me?

ARNAUD

I think she's sleeping, Grandmother.

MADAME CHARTRAIN

Completely unsettled. This is all going to end poorly.

ARNAUD

I hear the car. Do you want me to come to the station with you?

MADAME CHARTRAIN

Never in my life...

AMÉDÉE

I'm the one who'll put your grandmother on the train. Come on, Mama, the valise is on the front stoop. I'm surprised that Eveline isn't coming to take leave of you, Mama.

MADAME CHARTRAIN

You're surprised? I'm not. Besides, we saw each other at dinner. That's more than enough.

She exits, followed by AMÉDÉE *and* ARNAUD. *We hear the car leave.* ARNAUD *comes back into the room. He picks up a book, sits down.* EVELINE *enters softly.*

SCENE III

Arnaud, Eveline

EVELINE

Have they left?

ARNAUD

Yes, just now. I imagine you heard them.

A silence.

EVELINE

her voice trembling

Are you mad at me, Arnaud?

ARNAUD *gestures evasively.*

Do you blame me?

ARNAUD

I believe that, with excellent intentions…

EVELINE

I did evil?

ARNAUD

I'm afraid so.

EVELINE

vehemently

But I didn't have the right to let her go insane.

ARNAUD

Insane? What do we know?

EVELINE

So you don't understand that it's to get away, that it's out of despair that she wants to marry that boy who bores her—and that she'll be horrified tomorrow.

ARNAUD

You're so sure...about everything!

EVELINE

My poor Arnaud, you can't admit that experience is very solid. It's the only solid thing, even.

ARNAUD

You're right, I do refuse to admit that.

EVELINE

I suppose it's the opposite of what you call faith.

ARNAUD

I'd rather call it its location, but it doesn't matter.

EVELINE

For the rest of us, at any rate, a person doesn't have the right to underrate it. Experience, I mean.

ARNAUD

I understand. But it seems to me… I don't know how to explain myself…that you're too eager to think yourself responsible for others.

EVELINE

It's certainly easier to disengage from one's responsibility.

ARNAUD

I'm not so sure about that.

EVELINE

Think about it.

ARNAUD

What's difficult is not to assume it, to put it back.

EVELINE

I don't understand. I think that the temptation for the poor beings that we are is always to abstain, to let it be…

ARNAUD

You believe in action.

EVELINE

With my whole soul.

ARNAUD

You're probably right. But are you sure you see where she is?

EVELINE

We're just quibbling now…

ARNAUD

Oh! No, Eveline, you're mistaken.

EVELINE

So you're taking it upon yourself to approve of this marriage?

SCENE IV

The same, Maggie

MAGGIE

I've taken advantage of your husband being out to come say a word to you, Eveline. Bonjour, Arnaud. (*To* EVELINE) I waited for you until dinner.

EVELINE

Excuse me, Maggie, I couldn't go to see you. Stella isn't good at all today.

MAGGIE

indifferently

What's wrong with her?

EVELINE

And I'll even ask you to excuse me for a moment. I need to see if she needs anything.

MAGGIE

I only have a few minutes.

EVELINE

I'll be back right away.

She exits.

SCENE V

Arnaud, Maggie

MAGGIE

You seem very sad.

ARNAUD

Not especially.

MAGGIE

It's horrible!

ARNAUD

How's that?

MAGGIE

It's a way of recognizing that normally... Oh! I understand, life here has nothing gay about it. I often wonder how Eveline could do it. Besides—

She cuts off.

That's a riddle, too.

ARNAUD

But don't you think that we all move about among riddles... I don't know...like in a dark room, between furniture that we can't see and we're afraid of running into.

MAGGIE

Not at all. No, I don't have that impression at all. I'd find that intolerable.

ARNAUD

It's not something you choose.

MAGGIE

All the same. It must be said that Papa has such a clear mind—and that he's a marvelous educator. There aren't words to express everything I owe him. And then all the readings that he's had me do since I was twelve...

ARNAUD

Pen in hand, I imagine.

MAGGIE

You don't know how right you are. I've never read a book that was worth the trouble without taking notes. I'm not talking about novels. I detest them anyway. Another trait I have in common with Papa.

ARNAUD

You have very serious tastes.

MAGGIE

I just hate feeling like I'm wasting my time.

ARNAUD

That's very good.

MAGGIE

Once Eveline was like me. Since her marriage, I don't know... I've often noticed that marriage often corresponds with arrested development.

ARNAUD

What about for men?

MAGGIE

I don't know.

A silence.

You intrigue me so much...you have no idea of it!

ARNAUD

I'm sorry.

MAGGIE

Why?

ARNAUD

It must be an unpleasant sensation not to be able to put me in a box. No?

MAGGIE

Not only that. No, certainly not. And even, I'm going to confess something that will astonish you... I think of you very often. Do you know why? In my room, there's a reproduction of a knight that's in the museum in Antwerp,[3] you know it well. And I think that you look like him. Do you see what I mean?

ARNAUD

No, I haven't traveled very much.

MAGGIE

What joys you're depriving yourself of!

ARNAUD

I have no curiosity whatsoever.

MAGGIE

That's what I can't understand. Life is so short! How do you not feel the need, I don't know...to amass...

ARNAUD

Beautiful impressions?

MAGGIE

Beautiful memories, Arnaud, come on!

ARNAUD

That treasure—we won't take it with us.

3. Presumably the Royal Museum of Fine Arts Antwerp. Marcel may have in mind Jan van Eyck's *The Adoration of the Lamb* (*The Knights of Christ*) (1432).

MAGGIE

Where's that? You're so funny! Hey, for example, my father, during the winter nights, he rereads the guides to countries that he's visited, he looks at the postcards, the photos that he's brought back from his travels.

ARNAUD

It's a sort of inventory... That would make me sad.

MAGGIE

Not at all: it's exciting. Ultimately, I'll tell you, you live in a kind of tomb.

ARNAUD

I don't think that's true at all, Maggie. If you want me to use an analogy, I'd say instead that I live at sea...and you—you prefer terra firma.

MAGGIE

You're wrong about that, Arnaud. I love cruises.

SCENE VI

The same, Madame de Puyguerland

MADAME DE PUYGUERLAND

Bonjour, Arnaud… Mademoiselle… Alain isn't here?

ARNAUD

No, Madame. We haven't seen him since early afternoon.

MADAME DE PUYGUERLAND

I wanted to call you, I couldn't get through.

ARNAUD

I had to make a long call to Paris for my grandmother, who has just left us…

MADAME DE PUYGUERLAND

Entirely impromptu?

ARNAUD

Yes.

MAGGIE

getting up

Eveline isn't coming back down. Give her my best. I hope your sister isn't doing worse.

MADAME DE PUYGUERLAND

Stella? …

ARNAUD

She got up for a minute this afternoon, but she wasn't feeling well and had to lie back down.

MAGGIE

Au revoir, Arnaud. No, I refuse to find anything maritime in you.

ARNAUD *accompanies her to the door.*

SCENE VII

Arnaud, Madame de Puyguerland

MADAME DE PUYGUERLAND

Arnaud, I'm tormented…you can't even know.

ARNAUD

I don't think that's necessary, I assure you. You know perfectly well that Alain has always had the passion for long, spontaneous walks.

MADAME DE PUYGUERLAND

He gets tired much more quickly than before… At any rate, lately, I've felt him to be so on-edge, so anxious… You say that he came in the early afternoon. He didn't see Stella, of course?

ARNAUD

No. I know that he had a conversation with Papa and with Eveline.

MADAME DE PUYGUERLAND

Is your father here?

ARNAUD

He took Grandmother to the station, but I suppose it won't be long before he gets back. Eveline should come back downstairs soon.

MADAME DE PUYGUERLAND

You, Arnaud—you didn't see Alain?

ARNAUD

No.

MADAME DE PUYGUERLAND

You don't know if…

She doesn't finish.

ARNAUD

Here comes Eveline.

SCENE VIII

The same, Eveline

EVELINE

Has Maggie already left? (*To* MADAME DE PUYGUERLAND) Bonjour, Madame.

ARNAUD

Maggie asked me to tell you that she couldn't wait for you.

EVELINE

What a funny creature!

MADAME DE PUYGUERLAND

Excuse me for coming at this unjustified hour, but Alain hasn't come back. I had the vague hope I'd find him here. Arnaud told me that you saw him this afternoon.

EVELINE

That's right.

MADAME DE PUYGUERLAND

May I ask if he seemed particularly...preoccupied to you?

EVELINE *hesitates.*

I'm begging you, Madame, don't hide anything from me.

EVELINE

He was certainly very agitated. But I'm sure you know that since our conversation, he wrote a letter to Stella that she...

MADAME DE PUYGUERLAND

She called me. She'd wanted to speak to him. I'm sure it was about that letter. I told her that he was out. She told me that she'd come say hello at the end of the day. She didn't come. At any rate, whatever feelings Alain's letter inspired in her, he didn't know anything about them, since they weren't able to communicate today.

EVELINE

I'm sure...

MADAME DE PUYGUERLAND

What matters to me is to know exactly what state he was in at the end of that conversation.

EVELINE

Very agitated, I'll repeat. But the kind of quite...unreasonable exaltation he was in the grips of didn't stop him from writing that letter which could only have been a marriage proposal.

MADAME DE PUYGUERLAND

So what? What conclusions do you draw from that?

EVELINE

He hasn't decided to come back because he expects to find, upon his return, the response that will settle things definitively... Yes, he's delaying the decisive moment.

ARNAUD

That's very plausible.

MADAME DE PUYGUERLAND

You, Arnaud—would you act this way?

ARNAUD

We have such different natures, Alain and I.

MADAME DE PUYGUERLAND

Do you have reason to think that Stella has answered him?

ARNAUD

I'm sure she hasn't.

MADAME DE PUYGUERLAND

I couldn't see her?

EVELINE

I just ask you to wait a day or two. Her condition is tormenting me.

MADAME DE PUYGUERLAND

Her physical state, or her moral one?

EVELINE

It's impossible to distinguish between the two.

A silence.

MADAME DE PUYGUERLAND

Arnaud, do you have…some ascendency over Alain?

ARNAUD

Unfortunately, no. Not in the slightest.

MADAME DE PUYGUERLAND

You know he was a very pious child. And then, I don't know, his professors at the lycée, his friends, the things he read… Two years ago I thought I noticed a resurgence of fervor in him… I got him to talk with Abbé Furet two or three times. But I'm afraid that the abbé didn't know how to reach him. He discouraged him. You, my dear Arnaud, I've always had the feeling that if you could undertake—

EVELINE

What a terrible word!

MADAME DE PUYGUERLAND

You could get him to take up a religious practice again. He didn't want to go to Easter Mass. If he accepted communion, certain awful ideas would leave him.

ARNAUD

Do you mean…the thought of suicide?

MADAME DE PUYGUERLAND

low

Yes.

EVELINE

I think you absolutely should not take his threats tragically. I have the very clear impression that he's playing a game with them.

MADAME DE PUYGUERLAND

her voice trembling

Even if you were right—it's never charitable to talk that way...

EVELINE

On the contrary, it seems to me—

MADAME DE PUYGUERLAND

No, no. Besides, I'm not surprised...this game, as you call it, could be fatal in the long run.

ARNAUD

I've sometimes wondered if you shouldn't take him very far away, go on a long trip with him, to Egypt, to India...

MADAME DE PUYGUERLAND

So you're pretty sure that Stella will refuse?

ARNAUD

This afternoon, on the contrary, I saw her as having decided to marry him. But Stella is not in her normal state, Eveline told you that. She herself doesn't know what she wants. I think we need to give her the time to get ahold of herself again.

MADAME DE PUYGUERLAND

You're not taking stock of the circumstances, Arnaud. You're reasoning in the abstract. This trip that you're recommending, that would be torture for him. He almost can't stand me anymore. Most of the time, we eat our meals separately. You see, that's the consequence, I think, of a past that's been too heavy. Since my husband's death, you know, I've lived only for him. I didn't know how to hide it from him. He hasn't forgiven me for it. I read books by those psychologists...those psychoanalysts they talk about so much nowadays. But life is so much more complicated than they think it is, so much more terrible. Maybe Alain has a kind of passion for me...that's very possible. And that's even why he's remained single so much longer than the others. Oh! I'm too lucid...too lucid... But he's maintained a profound rancor toward me. Maybe he doesn't even suspect it himself. He only knows that I annoy him... It's not my fault. It's not his, either... I've often thought...yes, I've even told priests about it, only they didn't understand, they didn't want to...it's as if human suffering didn't have the right to go past certain limits. When it goes beyond them, it develops the same consequences as a serious fault. It's...castigated. If I'd been easily consoled over the death of my husband, there would have been other interests in my life. I wouldn't have weighed so heavily on my poor Alain. And now—

She stops talking, overwhelmed.

ARNAUD

profoundly softly

They didn't understand?

MADAME DE PUYGUERLAND

You mean the priests? No. It's so contrary to what they teach… Oh! They're surely right. I'm the one who thinks wrong.

ARNAUD

No. It's just that perhaps you're not going all the way there. This suffering you speak of, which goes beyond what nature admits… I imagine that it's not a fault, but a very heavy privilege, and that it has to be accompanied by a certain renunciation. Otherwise, it's self-indulgence. Illicit. Destructive. Not only for oneself: especially for others.

MADAME DE PUYGUERLAND

profoundly

That must be the truth… Thank you, Arnaud.

EVELINE

who hasn't been able to hide a certain annoyance

I ask you, Madame, to think of Stella. She's the one who we must be most concerned about right now. When I went up to her a few minutes ago, I found her feverish, almost delirious. If, as I fear, in that letter whose text we don't know, Alain is blackmailing her—

MADAME DE PUYGUERLAND

I'll ask you to take that word back.

EVELINE

Unfortunately, it's the only one that's suitable.

ARNAUD

Eveline, you're wrong. Remember—

EVELINE

to MADAME DE PUYGUERLAND

We have the strict obligation, you and I, to put Stella on guard against that...exploitation. Unconscious, I think, but even more dangerous because of that. And ultimately, in the current state of things, if Stella writes him, you have a duty to intercept her letter.

MADAME DE PUYGUERLAND

Madness!

EVELINE

You don't want to look reality in the face.

MADAME DE PUYGUERLAND

You yourself—are you so sure? ...

EVELINE

It's never frightened me.

MADAME DE PUYGUERLAND

But then... (*In another tone*) Did Amédée talk to Alain?

EVELINE

For a few minutes.

MADAME DE PUYGUERLAND

Does he share your...apprehensions?

EVELINE

You know Amédée: He's the center of his world.

MADAME DE PUYGUERLAND

What do you mean by that?

EVELINE

You know as well as I do that he's never had a feeling for other people.

MADAME DE PUYGUERLAND

I notice you haven't answered me. Arnaud…

ARNAUD

Papa has a lot of affection for Alain.

EVELINE

You know it perfectly well—a person doesn't have value for your father except in the image of himself that he sees at the back of their eyes. Provided it's flattering…

MADAME DE PUYGUERLAND

with a growing acerbity

Of course, you judge yourself entirely unscathed by that… weakness?

EVELINE

How's that?

MADAME DE PUYGUERLAND

And yet the invincible antipathy that I inspire in you...don't deny it...certainly comes from the fact that you haven't found in my eyes a reflection that satisfies you.

EVELINE

You're Amédée's friend. You've never cared to be mine, as far as I know. I remember quite well the first visit that I made to you on Boulevard de Courcelles[4]...

ARNAUD

Eveline, how do you not see that all of this is...more than painful?

MADAME DE PUYGUERLAND

The truth is that from the first day, you felt in my face a question that you didn't like.

EVELINE

What question?

MADAME DE PUYGUERLAND

Is it really necessary to formulate it?

EVELINE

What question?

4. A large street that runs from the eighth to the seventeenth arrondissement, past the Parc Monceau that Amédée and Madame de Puyguerland played twenty questions in as children.

ARNAUD

Madame, I ask you not to respond. Have the charity not to respond.

MADAME DE PUYGUERLAND

I suppose it's too late to call?

ARNAUD

It's after nine.

MADAME DE PUYGUERLAND

I'm going home. Alain is probably back.

ARNAUD

That's probably true… I'll call you tomorrow morning to be sure that everything is going well… But I'm not worried.

MADAME DE PUYGUERLAND

Thank you, my dear Arnaud. You're a good man.

ARNAUD

In fact, could I see you home?

MADAME DE PUYGUERLAND

No, I have my car. That's quite unnecessary.

She exits with ARNAUD, *who returns after a moment.*

SCENE IX

Eveline, Arnaud

EVELINE

bitterly

I hate it when you play the angel.

A silence.

So you're taking your part against me?

ARNAUD

I have a lot of affection for her.

EVELINE

I see that.

ARNAUD

And you yourself know that you're not being fair.

EVELINE

I've always felt such a partiality in her.

ARNAUD

No, Eveline, I don't think so. She wasn't asking for anything except to accommodate you.

EVELINE

Accommodate! What words you use…

ARNAUD

It's just, there's something she wasn't able to explain, and since she's very conservative…

EVELINE

She has all the qualities.

ARNAUD

Certainly not. Great virtues, and a profound weakness, but one she's aware of.

EVELINE

Ultimately, this question that you asked her not to ask me, do you yourself…?

ARNAUD

For a long time, I've wanted to turn my mind away from it. That's no longer possible for me, Eveline. And I even think that we don't have the right to do that anymore.

EVELINE

We?

ARNAUD

You and I.

EVELINE

Do you want to talk about what happened in Engadin?

ARNAUD

softly

About your marriage, quite simply... There's an unknown weighing on our lives. As long as you don't bring it to light, your devotion to Stella can only turn back against her.

EVELINE

I don't understand at all.

ARNAUD

I'm not certain I understand it, but I see it.

EVELINE

I envy your certainties.

ARNAUD

No, Eveline. A person can only envy possessions, and I don't have any. My destitution is absolute. And I myself, when I think about it, I sometimes feel a nameless sadness. Which proves...

EVELINE

Well?

ARNAUD

That there's nothing there that we have the right to look at.

EVELINE

I'd love to be in your position.

ARNAUD

That's another illusion. It's because you picture something that doesn't exist, or at least that a person can't imagine at all… (*A beat*) You don't want to try to explain it to me? … It's not out of curiosity, I assure you. It's a kind of anguish, but one that wouldn't be at all personal. An anguish for you.

EVELINE

slowly, deafly

You can't know the weeks of revolt that I'd spent since I got to Silvaplana. I told you that often, I had almost decided to leave my father, to leave for Vienna… I don't know why, Vienna attracted me at the same time it scared me. I told myself: I'll lose myself there, I'll lose myself there… I repeated that with a kind of tense, desperate satisfaction. It seemed to me that I didn't love anyone, that I'd seen through every feeling. Naturally, there was my unfortunate love for that doctor… Nothing remained of that but bitterness, a cinder I rolled around in like sand… And when I saw the two of you… I'll never forget that day at the end of July… at breakfast. And afterwards, the same day, when we met near Lej da la Tscheppa,[5] you remember that long walk back…it was as if my heart was beginning to live again. I wanted to laugh and to cry… I don't know… The two of you had entered into my life. Like into a sad room. You'd opened the curtains, the windows. The sun came in.

5. A lake in the Engadin Valley.

ARNAUD

But Eveline...

EVELINE

You didn't talk about your father immediately. Or at least you didn't describe him to me. I had a very vague idea of him, a little solemn, but one that I liked, or at least... And then there was an atmosphere around him... I don't know how to put it...a kind of decorum of the soul. Oh! I hate that now, but why won't I admit that I was fooled by it at first? Very quickly I understood that an idea had gotten into your heads, you and Stella, that it had taken root in you. You'd adopted me, you wanted me in your lives. I felt...picked up. Yes, that's it, I'd reached port. And I lived, during those few weeks, under the empire of a fixed idea: don't be disappointed. But for all that, I needed...to please him. And the only way to do that was not to look at him too much, not to let a disturbing truth that I was beginning to feel penetrate me entirely. A bit, you understand, like when you try not to breathe some odor. It's just that it's a comparison that hasn't come to me until just now...

ARNAUD's silence is weighing on her.

Are you judging me?

ARNAUD

No, I'm trying to understand, to remember...

EVELINE

In certain decisive periods, it's like on narrow, vertiginous roads:

you don't go forward except thanks to an instinct, except on the condition that you look...this way, but not that way. Especially not that way... And then I'd be lying if I didn't admit to myself that the respects he paid to me flattered me. Yes, my vanity. Up to that point I hadn't drawn anyone's attention except for rather mediocre people, or people who seemed insignificant to me. Friends of my father, very boring, technicians for the most part. Your father benefited, in my eyes, from a sort of odds...it's lamentable, but I think it's the truth. And it's because of the two of you, because I loved you, that I didn't want to be careful. You see, Arnaud, I don't think about myself.

ARNAUD

But him...did you happen...even once...to think of him?

A silence.

EVELINE

low

I don't know.

ARNAUD

Don't you find that rather...terrifying? You declared just now that he didn't have a feeling for other people... Was it your business to make that complaint?

EVELINE

acerbically

I'm begging you, Arnaud, don't be so terribly right. It doesn't feel like I'm talking to a human being... I'm trying to explain myself.

You understand, he's so concerned with himself, it's as if he dispensed you from putting yourself in his place.

ARNAUD

Are you saying that seriously?

EVELINE

intimidated

Yes, it seems to me I am.

ARNAUD

Concerned with himself... Did you ever come to the idea of thinking that that was the fact of a very weak being, very disarmed, but also very eager, very unhappy...

EVELINE

I don't know that your father is capable of suffering—what I'd call suffering.

ARNAUD

What you'd... You need your pain to be verified, Eveline. There are other types of pain, just as there exist illnesses that aren't recognized. And they're no less awful. For my part, I think that Papa is an extremely unhappy man, much unhappier because he communicates less with his pain. The kind of indistinct thirst that devours him—he himself doesn't know it—just because it's devoured him.

EVELINE

I don't know. That's one view of the spirit.

ARNAUD

It's a certainty. If you ever tried...to decipher him using this grid...but maybe it's too late.

EVELINE

I've never seen anything in your conduct toward your father that has ever betrayed that...surprising conviction. With him, you are deferential, but very distant. Basically, you treat him almost like a stranger.

ARNAUD

Do you think that I don't feel guilty toward him? He's like an island that I've never found a way to reach. Every day, I pray to do it. And then, Eveline, as bizarre as this seems, it's only now, by talking to you, that I've realized...his misery. It's so strange: You saw Stella's, you didn't discover his. And yet they're like each other, they're inseparable. And further—a little further, behind them, there's another unhappiness, another victim.

EVELINE

Yes, I know who you mean.

ARNAUD

It's just, Eveline... I beg your pardon, I'm going to seem very hard...it seems to me that a person doesn't have the right to make use of those who aren't there anymore, to enlist them... My mother, Eveline...that desperate act she must have rushed into the way a person throws himself into death...

EVELINE

Well?

ARNAUD

I've often wondered if it wasn't, in reality, my father who had breathed the idea into her ear.

EVELINE

What do you mean?

ARNAUD

Simply because he expected that she'd go through with it, because he needed it, you understand. As if he needed an event to occur in order to justify his self-pity to himself… Maybe those we call criminals are sometimes just…spellbound. But she couldn't recognize herself in that borrowed crime… I think that it separated her from herself. And that's why her mind was troubled…what she'd really lost.

EVELINE

Where does this light come from?

ARNAUD

We'll never know any more on this side of death. Be sure that she herself wouldn't have been able to explain anything—and him neither. As for me, I long ago made the commitment to accept this ignorance.

EVELINE

A commitment to yourself?

ARNAUD

No. It's a pact that I signed.

EVELINE

With whom?

ARNAUD

I don't feel the need to give a name to my...partner. I just know that it's a presence...not a human presence...someone whom I can't talk about, but for whom I am a thou. He is there. He stands guard.

EVELINE

Over you?

ARNAUD

For me. For us.

EVELINE

That's inconceivable. There's the internal mirage you've built your existence on!

ARNAUD *doesn't protest.*

Arnaud!

ARNAUD

Excuse me. I shouldn't have—

EVELINE

How can I recognize myself in this inextricable snarl? The more there emerges from you, I don't know...an authority that subjugates me, the more it seems to me that I'm listening to a foolish child. Is there the fabric of a saint in you—or are you nothing but a visionary? I'm alone, I'm lost.

ARNAUD *doesn't say anything. We feel that he is absorbed in silent prayer.*

What time is it? Why hasn't your father gotten back yet? ... It's as if we were outside of life... I don't hear anything... Won't you let me near you? To speak your language, which will never be mine, Arnaud, maybe...yes, maybe I've sinned out of pride. You see, I've come to it, I'm not holding out... The road that I've followed until now hasn't led me anywhere. I'd like to change my route. Since you have the light that has been refused to me, why won't you agree to guide me? I'd be docile...and humble, I assure you. And maybe I'd learn to be fairer toward him—since you think I've misunderstood him. And at the moment, I'm sure that you must be right. It should have been...it should have been...

She leans toward him.

(*With anguish*) Arnaud, why aren't you answering me? It's as if you had a fear you didn't want to tell me.

ARNAUD

You're wrong, Eveline. I don't have the slightest apprehension...

The phrase hangs suspended.

EVELINE

Why do I have the impression that you're not telling me everything you think?

ARNAUD

hesitantly

There's a big decision that I made some time ago...or rather... no. I'm not the one who made it. It was...meant for me. I ask you to accept it, Eveline...even if it surprises you, as I'm afraid it will...

EVELINE

weakly

Ah!

ARNAUD

I'm going to be entering orders in a few weeks.

EVELINE

in a sort of desperate cry

You don't have the right... How do you want...?

She feels ARNAUD looking at her.

(*Babbling*) You have to get married, Arnaud, to have children... This isn't possible... It's an aberration... I'll die from it.

ARNAUD

profoundly softly

Dying, Eveline...do you really understand what it is to die?

EVELINE

with a sort of concentrated violence

I'll die from it.

ARNAUD

For my part, since I've heard that judgment, I think I can see what it is...what it will be. Through death, we open ourselves to what we've lived on earth... I'm giving you the thought that nourishes me.

EVELINE

You're offering me words.

ARNAUD

Eveline, do you never wonder what you're living on?

EVELINE

bitterly

I'm like the others. I only survive on the condition that I don't wonder... (*Deafly*) You've broken me.

ARNAUD

No, I think that I've removed from you something that would have suffocated us.

A silence.

SCENE X

The same, Amédée

EVELINE

You're so late! It must be a ridiculous hour.

AMÉDÉE

The train was late, Eveline. The night's so magnificent—we take advantage of this moving moonlight too rarely—I came back on foot. You know me, I was walking briskly, absorbed in my reflections. But luck had it—you would say Providence instead, my dear Arnaud, and ultimately you wouldn't be wrong—that I saw a form leaning over the edge of the pond. I didn't recognize him right away. Obeying I don't know what impulse, I left the path, I approached. And what was my astonishment when I noticed that this benumbed dreamer was none other than Alain, oh yes, Alain! I softly put my hand on his shoulder. He turned around. I'll never forget the expression of fear and something like indignant surprise that I read in his eyes at that moment.

EVELINE

Indignant?

AMÉDÉE

Because I'd interrupted a tête-à-tête that was rather sweet, but also rather…agonizing.

EVELINE

He was sleepwalking.

AMÉDÉE

with irritation

He wasn't sleepwalking, Eveline. I really don't like to rebuild... he'd abandoned himself to that sort of rather perfidious enchantment that comes out of sleeping waters. I don't know if you remember that magical song, that melody from Mussorgsky, I think, that Marie-Estelle used to sing in a very captivating voice...

ARNAUD

But Papa, you don't mean...

AMÉDÉE

Yes, exactly. A few moments more, and that sad and charmed child would have slid into death... He himself agreed, moreover, after having torn him away from that...malevolent torpor with a few amicable but rough thumps, I asked him very affectionately to wait there, at that hour, next to the Carmes Pond. I don't remember the exact words that he used. I was quite agitated, I'm not defending myself... "I was trying," he more or less told me, "to make myself agree with things exactly enough so as to finally myself become...a thing...without regret, without protestation." I reprimanded him, as you can guess; I told him about the terrible pain that his gesture would have caused his exquisite mother for whom he was her entire life... He listened to me in silence, without really seeming to understand. Half of him was still out there, among the reeds of the pond. The other half followed me like a mechanism. I didn't stop, of course, until I'd put him in the hands of his poor mother, who was already crying out of worry. I can still hear the almost inhuman cry that she let out when she saw us appear in the gracious boudoir where she'd been waiting for the return of the lost boy for hours.

EVELINE

For a few minutes at the most. She spent part of the evening here.

ARNAUD

That doesn't matter, Eveline.

EVELINE

I hate it when people exaggerate.

AMÉDÉE

She prepared for him under my eyes a boiling Chinese tea into which she poured the value of two or three spoonfuls of rum. I even owed my body a full cup of that comforting beverage. I won't be able to close my eyes tonight, but that's not important at all. Our Alain won't pay for his imprudence except with a head cold, and even that our friend flatters herself that she will cut off with a few homeopathic granules.

EVELINE

All's well that ends well. But I don't understand why he didn't wait for Stella's response to the letter that he wrote this afternoon before taking this extreme resolution.

AMÉDÉE

That only proves, my dear Eveline—and who would dream of reproaching you for it?—the extent to which a certain logic of the passions remains foreign to you. The expectation, Eveline, the expectation… That ordeal whose end one doesn't dare wish for, since it could be the final disappointment…

SCENE XI

The same, Stella

EVELINE

How are you doing, my dear? I didn't think you'd get back up tonight.

STELLA

I slept very deeply for an hour. And I don't know...when I woke back up, I felt as if something fortunate had happened while I was asleep.

AMÉDÉE *smiles.*

(*To* AMÉDÉE) What a funny expression you have on, Papa!

AMÉDÉE

No, Stella. I only remark that there are...coincidences at which we would rightly marvel.

ARNAUD

Just imagine, while Papa was walking by the pond, he saw Alain, who was asleep on a stone. You know how easily Alain catches cold... Papa woke him up, shook him, took him to la Guérinière. Madame de Puyguerland was very tormented... Everything ended well, you see.

STELLA

Poor Alain! So much the better. I'll call him tomorrow morning.

AMÉDÉE

Yes, my dear.

STELLA

He'll be happy… He wrote me a letter.

AMÉDÉE

Yes.

STELLA

Arnaud, did you notice? … When he's happy, he looks like a little boy whom you want to take in your arms.

She cries silently.

ARNAUD

tenderly, low

Why are you crying, Stel?

STELLA

I don't know. Everything is so mixed-up…inextricably. In us. Outside of us. I think about Alain on that rock, fainting, desperate. I see him tomorrow happy, almost mad… I don't want to remember that he annoyed me, exasperated me so much… I'm crossing all that out, you understand…

ARNAUD

Yes.

AMÉDÉE

My poor children, all the same, there are privileged instants where an order comes into form, graspable only by the most delicate and the most demanding ear. (*Looking at* EVELINE) For less expert musicians, these ravishing chords remain imperceptible.

EVELINE

her voice trembling

If it's me you're looking at Amédée, you're mistaken. I hear, like you, a kind of melody…suspended…tearing…incomprehensible… (*Lower*) Arnaud, when you're out there, you'll pray, won't you, for whose who have no hope? Death doesn't hold anything in reserve for them…nothing…nothing…

ARNAUD

with a serious softness

You don't know, Eveline, you don't know yourself… Everything is in front of you.

STELLA

coming to him

What are you saying? (*To* EVELINE) Oh! I know everything you're thinking.

EVELINE

sorrowfully

I'm not thinking anything. I'm no longer judging.

STELLA

The great marvel!

ARNAUD

Stella!

EVELINE

I barely understand what's happened. Did anything happen?

AMÉDÉE *is drowsy. He murmurs, "...Not night...nothing important..."* EVELINE *looks at him. She shakes her head.*

ARNAUD

with a profound pity, his eyes fixed on his father

A little more time, and all these phrases that he's so enchanted with will be lost in the silence. This affectation that he's fooled by will fall from him. He'll be there alone, disarmed, defenseless, like a child who has been struck by sleep and who still holds his toy against himself. In the face of the living creature who pontificates and gesticulates, Eveline, if we only knew how to evoke the recumbent man of tomorrow!

They look at each other. EVELINE *is vanquished by tears. She leans over and kisses* AMÉDÉE *on the forehead as if perhaps one day, later on...*

PARIS, MORGAT

APRIL–JULY 1937

CLUNY MEDIA

Designed by Fiona Cecile Clarke, the Cluny Media *logo depicts a monk at work in the scriptorium, with a cat sitting at his feet.*

The monk represents our mission to emulate the invaluable contributions of the monks of Cluny in preserving the libraries of the West, our strivings to know and love the truth.

The cat at the monk's feet is Pangur Bán, from the eponymous Irish poem of the 9th century. The anonymous poet compares his scholarly pursuit of truth with the cat's happy hunting of mice. The depiction of Pangur Bán is an homage to the work of the monks of Irish monasteries and a sign of the joy we at Cluny take in our trade.

"Messe ocus Pangur Bán,
cechtar nathar fria saindan:
bíth a menmasam fri seilgg,
mu memna céin im saincheirdd."

Made in the USA
Monee, IL
25 May 2021

68644069R00118